Jensen

Jensen

Keith
Anderson

Foulis

Haynes ®

A **FOULIS** Motoring Book

First published 1989

Published by:
Haynes Publishing Group
Sparkford, Nr. Yeovil, Somerset
BA22 7JJ, England

Haynes Publications Inc.
861 Lawrence Drive, Newbury Park,
California 91320 USA

British Library Cataloguing in Publication Data
Anderson, Keith
Jensen. (General motoring).
1. Jensen cars, to 1987.
I. Title. II. Series
629.2'222
ISBN 0-85429-682-4

Library of Congress catalog card number 88-82499

Editor: Mansur Darlington
Printed in England by: J.H. Haynes & Co. Ltd

Contents

Introduction

To make the decision to write a book such as this is almost as daunting a task as the actual research and writing itself. However, every person I contacted with a plea for help was so eager to oblige that the resultant task was made much easier than it might have been.

The list of such people is virtually endless, and I cannot mention them all here. They all have my heartfelt thanks, but without the following people there would be no book and, may I say, probably not as much interest in the marque itself. Firstly I must thank Mrs Elizabeth Jensen, Richard Jensen's wife and still a committed enthusiast. As well as providing valuable photographs and illustrations, there were also numerous anecdotes and reminiscences that would have been unobtainable elsewhere. Eric Neale, the designer of the 541 and C-V8 series needed little prompting to provide copious notes detailing events dealing with his time at Jensens. The book is all the richer for Eric's enthusiasm. I must thank Ian Orford, the man that brought credibility back to the *Jensen* name, and whose strength of conviction resulted in a brand new Jensen becoming available once again. The new Jensen Car Company Ltd under the direction of G.H. Wainwright has a lot to thank Ian for, because he kept the 'legend' alive.

Photographic contributions were many, but I particularly must thank the Jensen Owners' Club – especially Clifford Oakes-Jones, Keith Cerrino, John Lane and Harry Hilton – and also Andrew Edwards, who provided photographs that I found unobtainable elsewhere.

This book is for my daughter Jennifer.

1

The Early Years

THE YEARS 1906 and 1909 were important ones in the history of the motor car, for these dates were, respectively, the years in which Alan and Richard Jensen were born. These two brothers were firmly to leave their mark on the British motor industry and the cars that they built were to become known the world over for their quality, performance and sheer unpretentious style.

The Jensens' father was the son of a family of Danish immigrants that had come to Britain in the nineteenth century. He had started a ship-broking business, later diversifying into importing family provisions and settled in Moseley, Birmingham where Alan and Richard were born. In their formative years, neither boy showed any interest at all in the family business. Alan, a sensitive young man, became absorbed in hobbies such as collecting birds' eggs and, even at this early stage, showed an enthusiasm for newness and innovation, illustrated by an active interest in amateur radio. Richard also showed an enthusiastic interest in innovation, but this was of a more mechanical nature. When he was at school he maintained his bicycle to a fanatical degree and had a voracious appetite for reading anything involving motor cars.

An incident in 1928 was to become the foundation of their future career. Alan was enjoying a friendly game of tennis at his local tennis club when his close friend, Cecil West, appeared at the wheel of his own home-built motor car. West had aptly named the car the 'Bitza' and had spent a good deal of time on its preparation; this was its first outing. Alan's first impressions of the creation was not good and, although too polite to tell West of his opinion, Alan nevertheless accepted a lift home. Alan felt that its performance, handling and, above all, appearance, left much to be desired. When they arrived at the Jensen residence, Richard Jensen ventured outside to see what all the commotion was about. The two brothers investigated the vehicle briefly, and then West departed in a cloud of smoke. Alan looked at Richard and, echoing the thoughts of the Packard brothers thirty years earlier, remarked: 'If we cannot do better than that then we will die in the attempt.'

This was a challege that was subsequently pursued with relish by the brothers. It was not a pipe-dream, however, for, since leaving school, both brothers had followed careers in the motor industry. Alan had been in apprenticeship with Serck Radiators for some years, gaining his experience working his way through the machine shops, radiator shop, their tube mill, marine cooler department and finally finished up in the drawing office. The

The Austin 7-based 'Jensen Special No 1'.

drawing office suited Alan very well; his father had always wanted to be an architect, but the family had prevented him from achieving his ambition. It is likely that it was from their father that Alan and Richard had inherited that sense of purity of line that would always distinguish their work. Richard had been apprenticed to Wolseley Motors but was soon to join Joseph Lucas.

Their immediate family had never owned a motor car, but with some expectation, the brothers designed and built a substantial garage at the side of the family home. Their father was very much against motorcycles, so he offered to help with their first acquisition, provided that it was a motor car. Alan recalled, 'It was a question of two motor cycles or a car between us. We went out one Saturday morning and bought a 1923 Austin 7 Chummy Saloon for £65 and were driven home on trade plates. We had it stripped down and on its side by the evening!'

The Jensens transformed this little car into what was to be retrospectively referred to as 'Jensen Special No 1'. Every night after they came home from the factories, they worked until the early hours of the morning, using a very simple tool kit. Their most complicated piece of equipment was a common belly brace which had cost them all of seven shillings and six pence. Lead formers were manufactured on which the V-section wings were beaten. Carl Skinner, the founder of SU, gave them two of his carburettors. The Chummy Saloon became a very low two-seater with the styling features in vogue at the time: cycle wings, louvred bonnet side panels and a boat-tail. Alan felt that the radiator was an important and profound styling feature, so he designed 'No 1's' radiator himself, basing his style on the 3-litre Sunbeam of the time.

Once this car was completed, the brothers were eager to try another project. They sold the two-seater for £120, and started to modify another Austin Seven. It was painted a very bright primrose yellow, and it immediately caught the eye of the man who had bought their original car. The brothers promptly swapped the two-seater back again for the primrose saloon. They then rebuilt the original car, improving the specification by replacing the cycle wings with long flowing wings and running boards. While testing a small alteration to the front suspension one evening, not far from their home, Alan was stopped by another motorist, driving a Standard. Alan at first was somewhat perturbed, thinking that something had fallen off his own car, but trepidation turned to delight when the stranger introduced himself as Arthur Wilde, and said that he worked at Standards. Mr Wilde was very interested in the little car that Alan was driving, and after many questions, answers and much discussion, Wilde revealed that he was actually the Chief Engineer at Standards and asked whether Alan and his brother would be interested in visiting his factory.

When Alan told Richard of this chance meeting, he became very excited as well. They accepted Wilde's invitation immediately and turned up on the appointed day with their own car. The Standard men looked at their car and they looked at what Standard was offering and how the cars were built. The Standard management asked the brothers if they could design and build a similar style of body on a Standard chassis. The Jensen brothers were only too willing to accept such a proposal, and shortly a Standard chassis was delivered to their home. This was in 1929. The result was 'Jensen Special No 2'. Alan Jensen wanted to give the car a certain amount of family resemblance to the Standard that the car was based upon, so he designed a radiator styled like the Standard Motor Company's current design but V-fronted. This very imposing feature of the car was the result of considerable time (and overtime) spent at Sercks Radiators by Alan. His foreman at Sercks had not kept a completely blind eye, however, and when the management were informed of his activities they immediately sent him a bill for £21, for materials used. Alan was summoned to the office of Sydney Purchase, the Managing Director, and was asked to explain himself. He did so, finishing with the plea that he could not possibly afford £21. Sydney Purchase paused, looked young Jensen straight in the eye: 'How will a nominal one pound do, Jensen?' Alan thanked him profusely and fled from the office!

The Jensen brothers had put a lot of thought and a lot of work into their second car. Standard was impressed, but as was to be echoed in succeeding years, went no further. One morning while he was at the Standard works, Alan met Monty Tombs, who was at that time the Midland editor of *The Autocar*. Alan recalls, 'Monty introduced me to Avon Bodies, Warwick, who invited me to join them to design a production model, supervise the building, road-testing and final inspection. I never got to join their drawing office – they had no drawing office!' It was thus that the 'Jensen Special No 2' became the basic prototype for the Avon-Standard two-seater and drop-head coupé.

In 1931, a friend of the Jensens, Arthur Clackett, introduced them to J.A. Patrick, who had earlier started a business named Edgbaston Garages Ltd. After learning a little about them, Mr Patrick invited the two Jensen brothers to join his firm. Alan left Sercks, Richard left Lucas and they started work with Edgbaston Garages, in Selly Oak, Birmingham.

The brothers immediately set about reorganising the business, restructuring the servicing side, offering night opening and later Sunday opening. They soon established a coachbuilding department and started building specials based on the current Wolseley Hornet. The brothers' success led to them being invited to join the board of directors. The name of the business was thus changed to Patrick Jensen Motors Ltd.

J.A. Patrick had originally founded Edgbaston Garages Ltd for his son, Joseph, and his son-in-law. When the Jensen brothers became directors there was the occasional disagreement with the original family board members. This was only to be expected, of course, but towards the end of that year (1931), an incident occurred that was to lead to the brothers' resigning from the board. Joseph Patrick was walking through the reception area one day when he overheard the conversation of a couple of regular customers. One customer asked the other if he was acquainted with either of the young Jensens. 'Yes', came the reply, 'I know one of them well enough to call him Pat.' Joseph Patrick was understandably rather upset at this statement, and after consulting with his father, called a board meeting the very next morning. The resulting rather heated debate caused both Jensen brothers to resign from the board forthwith; they left Patrick Jensen Motors Ltd that afternoon.

The brothers had, by now, something of a reputation in the Birmingham motor trade and it was not long before they were contacted by a friend, John Hathaway, who had been a fellow apprentice with Richard at Wolseley Motors. Hathaway introduced them to George Mason, the son of a large provisions merchant. Mason senior had a financial interest in an old established coachbuilding firm, W.J. Smith & Sons. Smiths had been producing delivery vans for Mason, but he was not happy with the quality of these vans or with that of the coachbuilt vehicles produced for other customers. After discussions, the Jensen brothers joined the firm as joint managing directors to reorganise the business and to start sports car production. When they moved into Smith's premises at Carters Green, West Bromwich, the Jensens met the workforce, which numbered sixty at that time. Little did they know that many of their new employees were to stay with them for many years and become firm friends. Stan Miller joined W.J. Smith & Sons in 1920 and retired from Jensen Motors Ltd in 1967; J.B. Stevenson joined Smiths in 1928 and then served as Company Secretary of Jensens until 1964. The foreman of the body-building shop, Harry Cottell, joined Smiths in 1927. He was to become a trusted friend of the Jensen brothers and retired from their company in 1971.

William James Smith, who had founded the company sixty one years earlier, was now aged eighty-six and was still spending time at the works. He was to retire a few months later, however. Richard started to reorganise the business side and Alan started to pull the shop-floor together. From the time he joined Smiths Alan provided all the necessary drawings to produce cars and commercial vehicles, without, as he took great delight in remarking, the facilities of a drawing office.

There was a lot to be rectified with their new factory before the brothers could begin to think about car production. The workforce were very skilled but the methods they used and the tools and equipment installed were rather outdated and in rather poor repair. Alan, forever the designer, started to bring the production methods up to date. He redesigned the equipment, and the workers started to produce better jobs in a fraction of the time. He designed new commercial bodies and his first coach body weighed half-a-ton less than their previous ones.

The turnover of the business in 1931 was just over £22,000, which reflected the depressed financial climate of the day. Alan and Richard realised that, as new methods introduced by new management may not be very popular with the

Early days for the Jensen brothers at W.J. Smith & Sons Ltd, Carters Green.

shop floor, they would have to think very carefully about ways of improving that turnover. Alan's practical design work and Richard's prudent business sense were not the only factors in their future success, the atmosphere and team spirit that the two brothers achieved within the firm was soon reflected by the workers. Browning and Blunsden, in their book *The Jensen Healey Stories* illustrated this management/shop-floor relationship with this recollection by Harry Cottell:

'We had built a rather super coach for a chap named Everton in Leicester. The job had been finished in rather a hurry because he wanted to take delivery before a bank holiday. In those days all the commercial vehicles had to be measured by the local authority, and I remember Stan Miller, our foreman mechanic, driving this new coach down to the measuring place in the town, with Mr Alan sitting proudly in the back. When we got there the measuring tape was duly produced and we were dumbfounded when the Traffic Commissioner turned to Mr Alan and said, "Mr Jensen, your vehicle is three inches too long". The regulations stipulated an overall length of no more than 27 ft 6 in, but it turned out that this particular chassis overhung the front axle three inches more than normal. None of us had noticed, but it was made quite clear that the vehicle would not be accepted as it was.

'There seemed to be nothing we could do but take it back to the factory, work all night, and cut three inches out of somewhere. And that is exactly what we did, with Mr Alan and Mr Richard staying up all night to bring us beer and fish and chips. We took three inches out at the rear, a section was removed from the body, and all the seats inside were shuffled forward. The fellow couldn't believe it was the same coach when we took it back to be measured again in the morning. Needless to say, the customer never knew!'

Some interesting examples of W.J.Smiths' work before the Jensen brothers became involved.

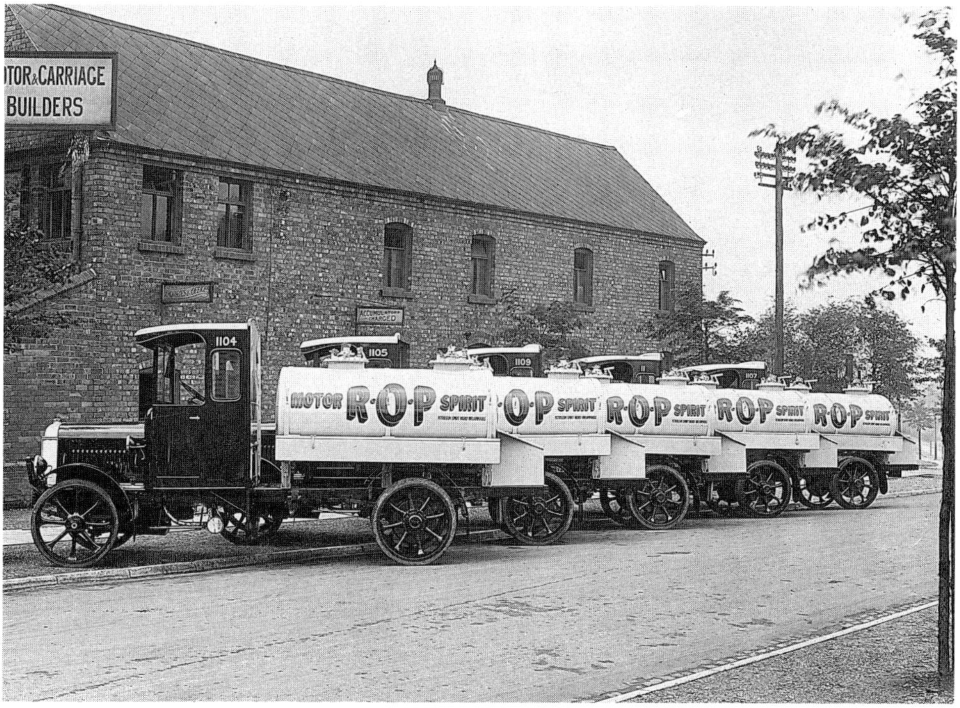

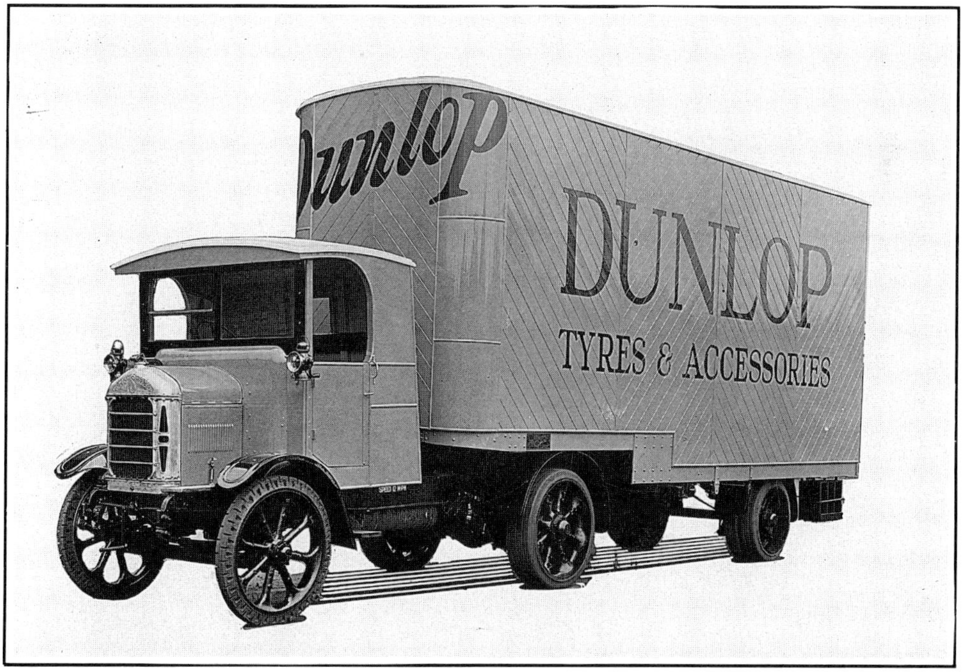

Alan Jensen's forte was drawing and design; therefore he had plenty to occupy his time with the commercial vehicle side of the business. Richard, still the keen motor car enthusiast, found a vacant corner of the factory and put this to good use for building car bodies. Alan recalled later that one of the reasons they had accepted the offer to join Smiths was that they would have the opportunity to start sports car production. Three years later, in 1934, the Jensen Brothers fulfilled their ambition and the company's name was changed to Jensen Motors Ltd.

At first, Jensens produced bodywork conversions on readily available chassis such as Morris Eight, Singer, Standard and Wolseley. As has been recorded before, Richard stated his formula for the Morris Eight conversion:

'The chassis from Morris cost us £125 and we charged £40 for the new bodywork, £20 materials and £20 for our labour and profit. The finished vehicle retailed at £225. This type of job was very successful, although we could never really compete with William Lyons's Swallow-bodied Austins and Wolseleys.'

As was to be demonstrated many times in the future by Mr Lyons and his magnificent Jaguars, it would be virtually impossible for any manufacturer, small or large, to try and compete with a product of such style, quality, performance and astonishing value. Wisely, the Jensens chose not to try, deciding to apply their skill and enthusiasm to sporting cars of an altogether more expensive class.

This emphasis on producing such exclusive cars was not to go unnoticed and the name Jensen was soon to be heard uttered by some of the world's richest and most successful people. One such person was Clark Gable, who at the time was considering purchasing a new car. Gable required a vehicle that was not just a means of transport, it had to be obviously expensive; it had to be rare and very exclusive; it had to have exciting performance. Above all, the car had to underline his own image: it had to have *style,* and bags of it. Therefore, Gable asked Jensen Motors Ltd to build him a special body on the Ford V-8 chassis. The brothers were only too willing to accept this commission, and shortly a pair of Ford chassis were on their way from Detroit.

The Jensens designed a car that fitted Gable's requirements admirably. It was a large, open four-seater, with long flowing front wings, the spare wheel in a cover and mounted behind the boot panel. For such a large and heavy car (by British standards), the styling was svelte, helped by a trim strip which continued the line of the bonnet edge back across the doors and swept down to the rear wheel-arch, coupled with the cut-out of the door following this line. The rear wings echoed the front with their swept-back lines. The car was a magnificent achievement. The brothers were justifiably proud of their creation and felt sufficient confidence to show it at the 1934 Ford Motor Show at London's Albert Hall before it was shipped out to the US. The car was a sensation at the show and enquiries came in from prospective customers about replicas being built. The Jensens would have been happy to oblige, but the chassis was effectively unobtainable: the Ford Motor Company never gave permission for their components to be used by another manufacturer for production models. Jensen had actually built two cars to the Gable specification and they were both sent off to America, the other car for a dealer. It turned out that Clark Gable didn't like the colour of the car intended for him and all photographs of him with *his* car actually show the other (dark blue) car. After a period of using the car he decided he wanted something ever larger and more imposing; he gave the Jensen back and ordered a Duesenburg. Both Jensens were subsequently sold by the dealer. The dark blue car is now owned by Warren Wyman in California and is kept in magnificent *concours* condition.

Clark Gable poses proudly with his Jensen.

The svelte lines of the Gable car made it instantly appealing.

Back in England customers were still enquiring about replicas. One of Richard's good friends was the pioneer aviator and racing driver, Lord Brabazon. When Brabazon heard of the Gable car's interest and the predicament that this had caused the Jensen brothers he promptly arranged for them to be introduced to Edsel Ford, Henry Ford's son. Edsel came across the Atlantic to sample the car and discuss the situation. He knew what to expect in driving the car but he was highly impressed with the styling and the quality of the hand-built construction. After talks with Alan and Richard, Edsel decided that the brothers were onto a winner and offered to supply their company with the required chassis, engines and spares back-up. The cars subsequently built were thus Jensen-Fords, in reality Fords with coachbuilt bodywork by Jensen of West Bromwich. They were very successful and about twenty 'Gable-Replicas' were produced, being sold by the Birmingham Ford dealers, Bristol Street Motors.

It was of the Jensen-Ford that Sir Malcolm Campbell wrote: 'I have nothing but praise: this car is something out of the ordinary, particularly noticeable to someone like myself who is continually driving all kinds of different makes.'

Richard and Alan were very happy with their arrangement with Fords, as it was a very lucrative profit-earner for their company. This success drew the brothers another step closer to their dream of being manufacturers of an exceptional motor car bearing their own name.

One of the stylish 'Gable Replicas' showing the lines of the raised hood.

2

The White Lady

NINETEEN THIRTY-FOUR was the year in which the Jensen brothers started to design the prototype that was intended to be the first production Jensen. The brothers had originally decided that their first car should be a four-seater tourer, with high-quality bodywork, exciting styling and excellent performance, which would again be provided with Ford's 3.6 litre V-8 engine. The effort put into designing the new chassis and styling the body, and the thought that was put into special features which would give the car a truly luxurious specification, were handsomely rewarded in the finished product. The Jensen family affectionately named this first car 'The White Lady'.

The chassis for the White Lady (this was only a family name, it was never a model name) was built to the Jensen design by Rubery Owen. The main chassis members were not the usual channel-section but were boxed and braced with a robust cruciform centre section. Added to this, a steel platform actually formed the floor of the car and extended from the A-pillars right back to the rear cross-member. This floor panel was welded to the chassis frame, making an extremely strong and very rigid assembly. The suspension was of half-elliptic leaf springs at front and rear, with the rear axle additionally located by radius arms running diagonally to the central cruciform. The Ford engine was to standard specification except for the two SU carburettors mounted on an alloy inlet manifold. The standard Ford three-speed gear-box was included, but again, in the interests of innovation, the brothers chose to fit a Columbia dual-speed rear axle. The idea of this type of axle was mainly to provide a high overdrive gear, but it effectively provided the driver with six forward gear ratios. The control for the dual axle was mounted on the dashboard fascia. This control operated a vacuum valve on the axle casing which, in turn, engaged a dog-clutch that controlled an epicyclic gear fitted between the bevel gear and the axle half-shafts.

The Jensens had achieved their intention of a car of style and performance; the White Lady had a long, low bonnet line and even longer flowing front wings. Alan designed a beautiful V-sectioned radiator grille that was destined to become as much of a trade mark of a Jensen as the famous radiators of Rolls-Royce and Bentley. In 1934 the car could perform well by the standards of the day: a top speed of 90 mph and a 0 – 60 mph time of just under 19 seconds. It was quite an achievement!

Richard and Alan Jensen looked long and hard at their creation, as regards its suitability as a production model. They realised that in some respects they

The original White Lady.

had sacrificed practicality for pure style, and after taking advice, they decided that if they were to produce a car of the type that they wanted to bear their name, that would also sell successfully, then one or two changes would have to be made. Their next prototype was to be the 3½ Litre Jensen, or the 'S' type.

This model was originally conceived as a traditional four-door saloon and was ready for 1935. The technical specification was the same as the White Lady, but the new body weighed quite a lot more, and this did affect the performance, although not by enough to discourage potential buyers. Again quoting Sir Malcolm Campbell, this time writing in the magazine *The Field*, 'I have never seen such attention paid to minute details as in the case of the 3½-Litre Jensen.

The first Jensen production model – The S-type.

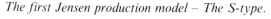

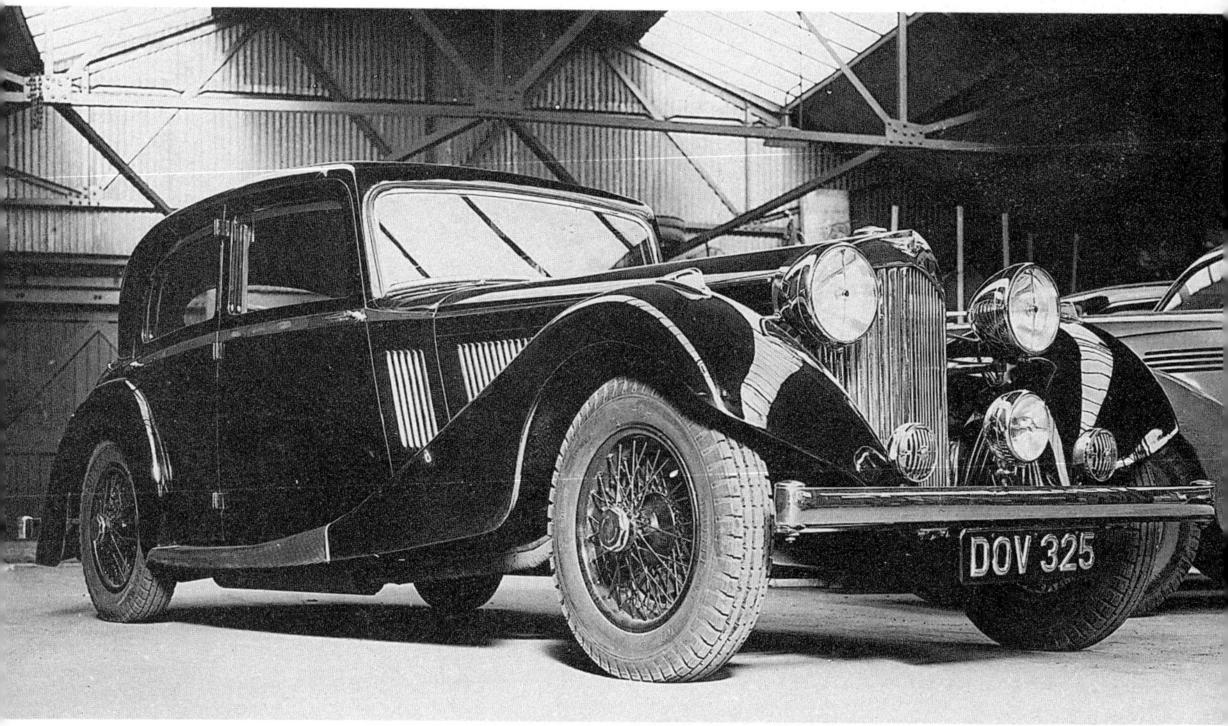

Every single point seems to have received careful attention, and it is possibly because of the great care that has been taken in the design that the car has a character all of its own. I have nothing but praise for the road performance of this car. The motor runs smoothly over its entire range and vibration is conspicuous by its absence. The appearance and the interior comfort of the Jensen leave nothing to be desired, I have no hesitation in giving the makers full marks.'

The prototype was exhaustively tested, modified and retested and it was at last put into production (albeit on a limited basis) later in 1935. To restore performance, the V-8 engine came in for modification by the Jensen factory.

Edsel Ford visits Jensens in 1935. The Jensen S-type is in the foreground with the White Lady in the background.

The original cylinder heads were replaced by heads cast in light alloy and the compression ratio was raised. Carburation was changed to two SU downdraught carburettors with an appropriate manifold. The usual Ford coil ignition system was replaced by a Scintilla Vertex magneto. The exhaust manifolds were redesigned and led into two separate exhaust systems. This treatment raised the power from the 85 bhp of the original engine to a more impressive 120 bhp.

Two photographs showing the extremely high quality interior of the S-type Saloon.

This production S-type was road tested by *The Motor* in October 1936. 'First Description and Road Test Report of an interesting eight cylinder car of high performance. Good Suspension. Liveliness and quiet running are features' was the heading of the article. The magazine went into their usual detail, but were not short of praise:

> The Jensen is undoubtedly good looking. In the tail there is a compartment for luggage and the spare wheel is mounted on the lid of that locker. Inside the car are two bucket seats and a wide rear seat with a folding central armrest. Leg room and head room are plentiful for all the occupants.
>
> Internally and externally the Jensen is very well finished. The woodwork is of polished walnut and the upholstery is of furniture hide with Dunlopillo squabs and cushions. These latter are particularly comfortable and in that connection it is worth noting that the bucket seats in the front are adjustable for angle as well as position. There are four concealed ash-trays, one at each end of the fascia-board and in each armrest at the ends of the rear seats. Above the screen is a clock, which can be seen easily by all the occupants of the car, and the other instruments are arranged so that they are nicely visible from the driving seat. There is a rev-counter as well as a speedometer, both having large dials. Neat and ingenious is the arrangement of the Philco radio set which can be fitted at an extra cost of £21.
>
> On the road the outstanding features of the Jensen 3½ Litre models are steadiness, silence and liveliness. The suspension system is undoubtedly good. Although soft enough for comfort, there is no suggestion of rolling on corners. Speed on this car is deceptive. Even when 90 mph was shown by the speedometer, there was no suggestion that the engine was finding things difficult.
>
> In short, the Jensen 3½ Litre is a Jekyll and Hyde car. It combines manners and appearance of a fine town carriage with the performance of the most brazen sports car.

Strong words indeed! The Jensen brothers had made their mark on the British motor industry. The praise of the press and of their customers, and the fact that the cars were selling well, encouraged the Jensen brothers and they decided to put a revised version of the original White Lady on the market. One of the revisions was to the front wings: the original design called for very long, flowing, open wings, but these proved to be capable of throwing mud in every direction possible. They were replaced with more enclosed, deeper front wings. The price of this model in 1936 was £645, the saloon model £695. *The Autocar* in their road test, number 1203 (17th June 1938), provided the following data:

Price:	With open four-seater tourer body: £645. Tax: £22, 10s
Rating:	30 h.p. 8 cylinders, side valve, 3622 cc capacity
Weight:	Without passengers: 30 cwt
Tyre size:	6.00 x 17 ins, on centre lock wire-spoked wheels
Lighting:	12 volt, automatic voltage control

Tank capacity:	20 gallons; approx fuel consumption: 17 to 20 mpg
Turning circle:	(L & R) 43 ft.
Ground clearance:	8″
Acceleration:	0 to 30 mph: 4.4 sec
	0 to 50 mph: 11.4 sec
	0 to 60 mph: 19.2 sec
	0 to 70 mph: 29.7 sec
Speed:	Mean maximum speed over 1/4 mile: 84.1 mph
	Best timed speed: 89.1 mph
Brake test:	Mean stopping distance from 30 mph (dry concrete) 27 feet

The Jensen brothers were never to rest on their laurels, however, and were constantly striving to perfect their product and introduce better methods of production, more efficient mechanical components etc. To this aim, Richard Jensen, after holidaying in Germany, was impressed with the performance and uncanny smoothness of the 2.2-litre Steyr. He subsequently imported four rolling chassis which the factory built into a four-door, four-seater open tourer design. These cars were exhibited at the 1938 London Motor Show, but did not actually go into production, for before long the two companies would find themselves in direct competition.

Political events notwithstanding, Richard turned again to the USA in his quest to improve his cars in the aspect of mechanical refinement and innovation. He was fascinated by the Nash 4.2-litre straight eight-cylinder engine. This engine offered very smooth performance with a refinement that was not equalled by the Ford V8. He fitted a Nash engine into a five inch longer chassis, this new model being called the 'H'-Type. At this point he took the opportunity of introducing independent front suspension. This Nash engine really was 'state-of-the-art' in 1938. The secret of its smoothness and refinement was its nine main bearings coupled with a dual ignition system that included twin spark plugs per cylinder. The cylinder block was cast integrally with the crankcase and push-rods operated the twin overhead valves per cylinder.

On 25 October 1938 *The Motor* stated its opinion of the idea behind the production of a car such as the H-Type Jensen. 'It is felt that the man who is prepared to pay a fairly high price for a car is entitled to expect that he may use it to the best possible advantage no matter what the road conditions may be. Similarly, it is fair to presume that such a buyer may wish to do quite a lot of his motoring on the Continent or still further overseas. Conditions encountered in this country are so much less severe than those to be found elsewhere, that the Jensen has been designed to cope with all emergencies.'

In 1939 the brothers felt that enough improvements had been introduced to merit a new model name. The 'HC'-type had coil-spring rear suspension and the later 'Continental' touring saloon had twin spare wheels mounted in the front wings to allow extra luggage space, as well as adding to the style. Three of these HC-types were built utilizing the 4.3-litre Lincoln V12 engine. This was again an effort to produce the latest in refinement. However, the Lincoln engine proved to be unreliable, echoing George Brough's experience. The Jensen brothers would not entertain this, of course.

Major Weir, the Sales Manager with the S-type Tourer.

The imposing front of the S-type.

S-type Drop-head Coupé with Molly Mason, wife of George Mason, who had introduced the brothers to W.J. Smith's.

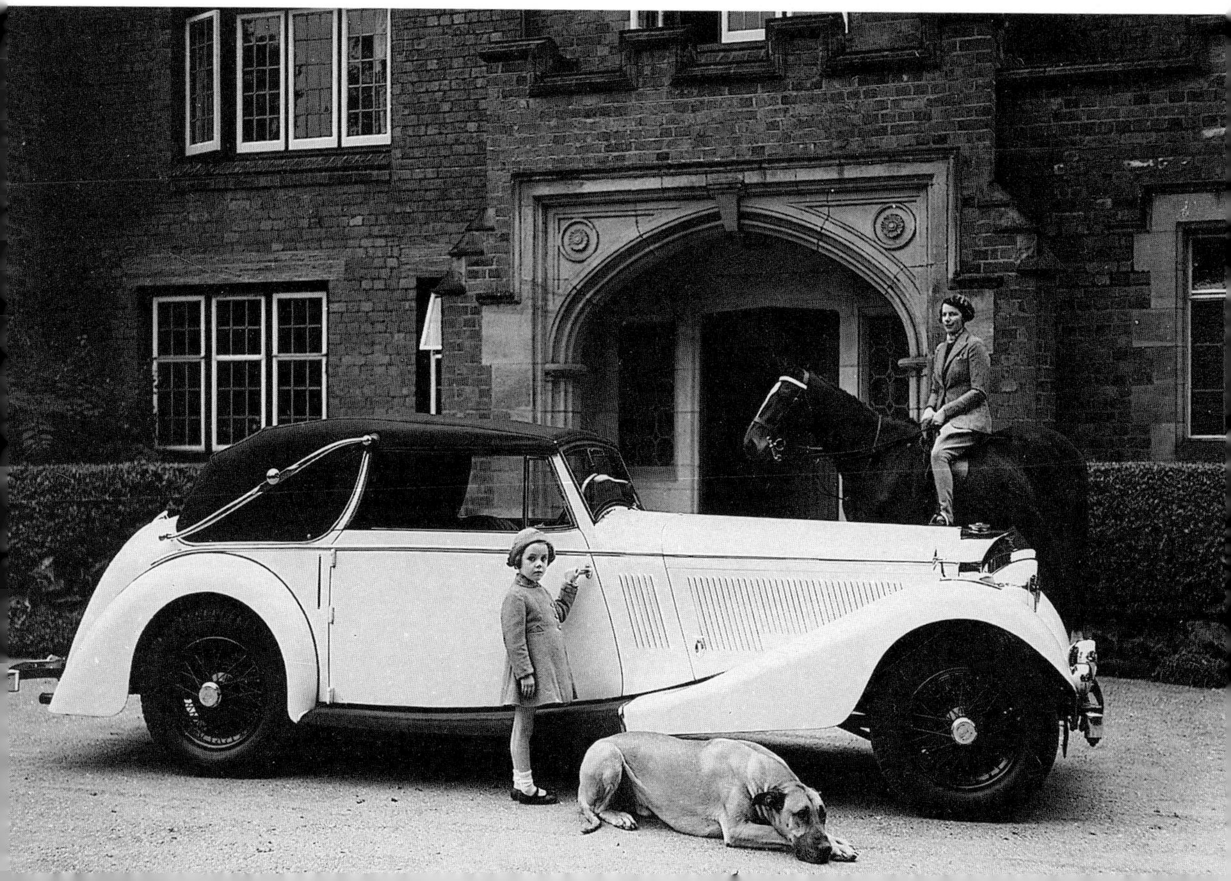

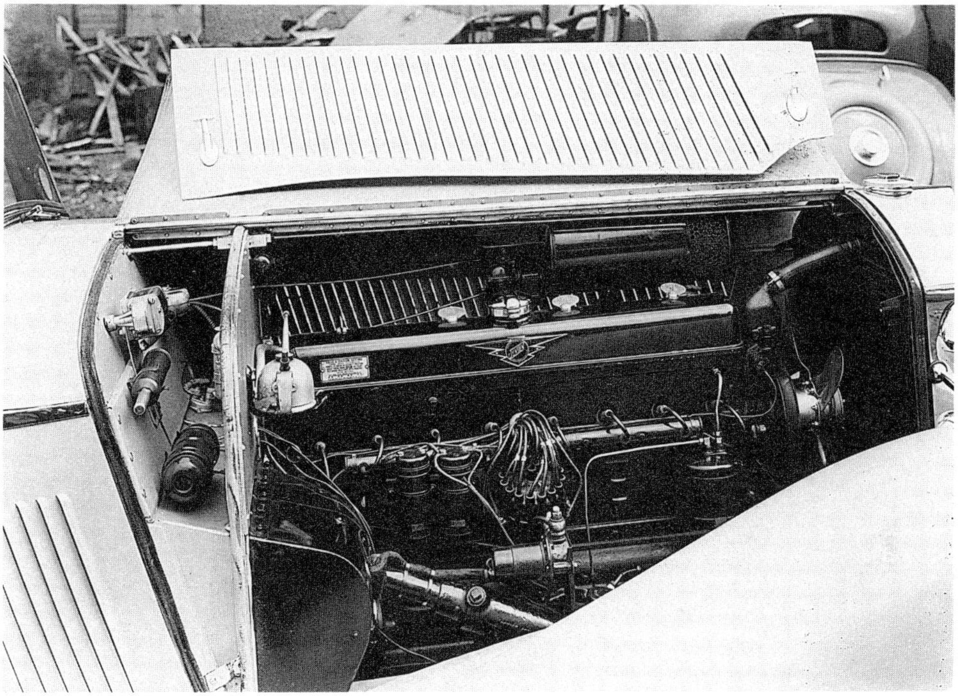

Jensen H-type engine bay showing the Nash straight eight-cylinder engine. Note that this engine had two spark plugs per cylinder.

H-type and S-type models featured on the covers of The Motor *and* The Autocar

Despite this success, the two brothers were soon off on another track. In the mid-1930s aircraft designers had just begun to accept aluminium alloy for structural purposes, recognising the material's capacity for giving lightness to a structure as well as great strength. It was this realisation of the advantages of aluminium which was to put Jensen Motors Ltd in the forefront of commercial vehicle technology in the years to come.

H-type with S-types as shown at the 1938 Earls Court Motor Show.

3

The Commercial Vehicles

IN THE LATE nineteen-thirties considerable interest was being taken in the use of the high-strength light alloys in the construction of commercial vehicles. In most cases, however, attention centred on the body of the vehicles, utilising the normal steel box-section chassis. In those days the law imposed limitations on the unladen weight of commercial vehicles and also restricted the speed of those weighing over 50 cwt. It took a company that was not afraid of introducing new and hitherto untried ideas to make use of the obvious advantages of light alloy in the construction of the whole vehicle. This company was Jensen Motors Ltd.

A customer of Jensen's, the Reynolds Tube Company Ltd, a subsidiary of Reynolds Rolling Mills, based in Tyseley, Birmingham, were faced with the problem of transporting loads of light alloy and steel materials, consisting mainly of long lengths, over long distances quickly and without damage. To solve the problem, Reynolds required a vehicle that would weigh less than 50 cwt, which would enable it to travel at the permitted speed of 30 mph (vehicles of over 50 cwt were limited to 20 mph). This vehicle would have to be capable of carrying long loads as well, and this was where the problem lay.

Reynolds turned to Jensen Motors Ltd, and Jensen and Reynolds subsequently collaborated over the design of an entirely new type of commercial vehicle. It had a body length of 27 ft 5 in – long enough for the load requirements – but had an unladen weight of just over 46 cwt – light enough for the Government speed restrictions. To achieve these remarkable specifications, the entire vehicle, with the exception of the engine, transmission, wheels and springs, was built of light alloys, its load capacity being four tons. It was the first commercial vehicle of unit construction, there being no separate body and chassis. The alloy Hiduminium RR56 was used for the structural members, and Hiduminium 45 for the flooring and plating sheets. The first vehicle was placed into service with Reynolds in February 1939. It was known as the JNSN four-tonner, and its registration number was AEA 200.

When the JNSN first appeared there was a school of thought that denigrated this new idea, it being believed that the construction would not stand up to the vibrations and wear and tear of normal road use, and that the structure would soon corrode. These prophecies were soon to be dismissed, however, as the new vehicle was covering some 800 miles per week with no problems whatsoever. The cost of the complete vehicle worked out less than that of a similar sized chassis with built-on body of equal capacity but higher unladen weight.

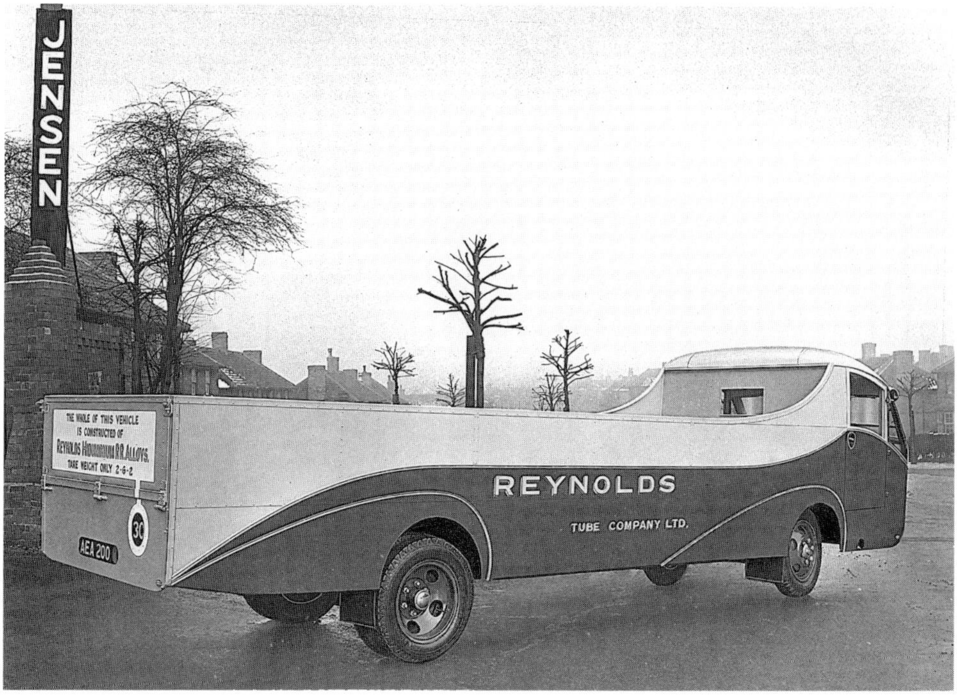

Two of the three light alloy vehicles built for the Reynolds Tube Company.

It was soon evident that the experiment was a resounding success. The Jensen brothers had called on their years of experience in coachbuilding commercial bodies (and the experience of W.J. Smiths before them) together with their flair for design, and the metallurgical capabilities of Reynolds. In the meantime a demand for still longer lengths of light alloy materials had arisen and it was decided to build a second vehicle, this time to take lengths of up to

30 ft, still having an unladen weight below the 50 cwt limit. This vehicle was a six-wheeler designed to carry five tons, and was placed into service in October 1939. The construction was almost identical to the first, with the exception of the necessary modifications required for the second rear axle, and the restyling of the front cabin.

A third vehicle was soon commissioned, but due to the wartime constraints on materials use was built slightly differently from the first two. The restrictions on the use of light alloys that came into being dictated the latest version could not be completed entirely in that material. The floor, cabin and sides were built in steel-faced wood, nevertheless the unladen weight was still a good two hundred-weight below the 50 cwt limit. It went into service in January 1940.

The original JNSN was designed to take the ubiquitous Ford V-8 power unit, but later versions used the 70 hp 4.7-litre Perkins P6 diesel. This was coupled to a British Moss five-speed gearbox with an overdrive. Another useful feature of this design was that the engine could be removed in less than thirty minutes by detaching the large front body panel.

In November 1942, the commercial vehicle magazine, *Transport World*, stated: 'All three vehicles have been in continuous service since being first commissioned. No replacements have as yet been found necessary to any of the aluminium members through failure or wear. All have been re-engined twice. Tyre wear has been less than normal for vehicles of this type and carrying capacity. The two four-wheelers are now using their second set.' The article went on to illustrate the merits of the JNSNs, their economical running costs and, in the final event of their being discarded, how each would have a very high scrap value. This last advantage would not be realised for many years however, as by the early 1960s, the first JNSN had logged over 750,000 miles!

The experience gained with these vehicles proved beyond any reasonable doubt that light alloys, provided that they are used correctly in design, could stand up to very severe conditions of service. The JNSN in its many forms over the years brought the company as high a reputation in the world of commercial vehicles as the S and H-types had achieved with the motoring world. The commercial body-building side of the business had been the backbone of the firm's finances right from the beginnings with W.J. Smiths, and accounted for a significant share right up until the 1960s.

The specifications of the first three JNSNs made for Reynolds were as follows:

Type	*Engine*	*Capacity*	*Unladen Weight*	*Average mpg*	*Date into Service*
JNSN four-wheeler, AEA 200	Ford V8	5 tons	46 cwt 66 lbs	12.1	February 1939
JNSN six-wheeler, AEA 978	Ford 4-cyl, 24 hp	4 tons	49 cwt 73 lbs	12.56	October 1939
JNSN four-wheeler, FOA 823	Ford 4-cyl, 24 hp	4 tons	48 cwt 35 lbs	13.78	January 1940

These three shots show the devastation suffered by the Jensen factory in the blitz of November 1940.

With the outbreak of war, Jensen were obliged to shelve most commercial vehicle production and all sports car production. Like most other motor vehicle factories they turned to military production, manufacturing simple although essential items such as aircraft seats, bomb casings, barrage-balloon facings and other suchlike components absorbed voraciously in an all-out war effort. Their specialist skills were not to go unnoticed, however, and they were soon engaged in the production of specialised military vehicles, ambulances and fire-tenders as well as revolving gun turrets for tanks and armoured cars. Later in the war, the Jensen brothers helped to overcome problems in converting the Sherman Tank for amphibious use in preparations for the D-Day invasion of Europe.

Some Jensen war jobs: Bombs and bomb-crates and a Jensen load ready for delivery.

Special bodies for the RAF. Mobile fire pumps for the NFS.

Control turntables for tanks during manufacture.

A completed control turntable for a tank . . .

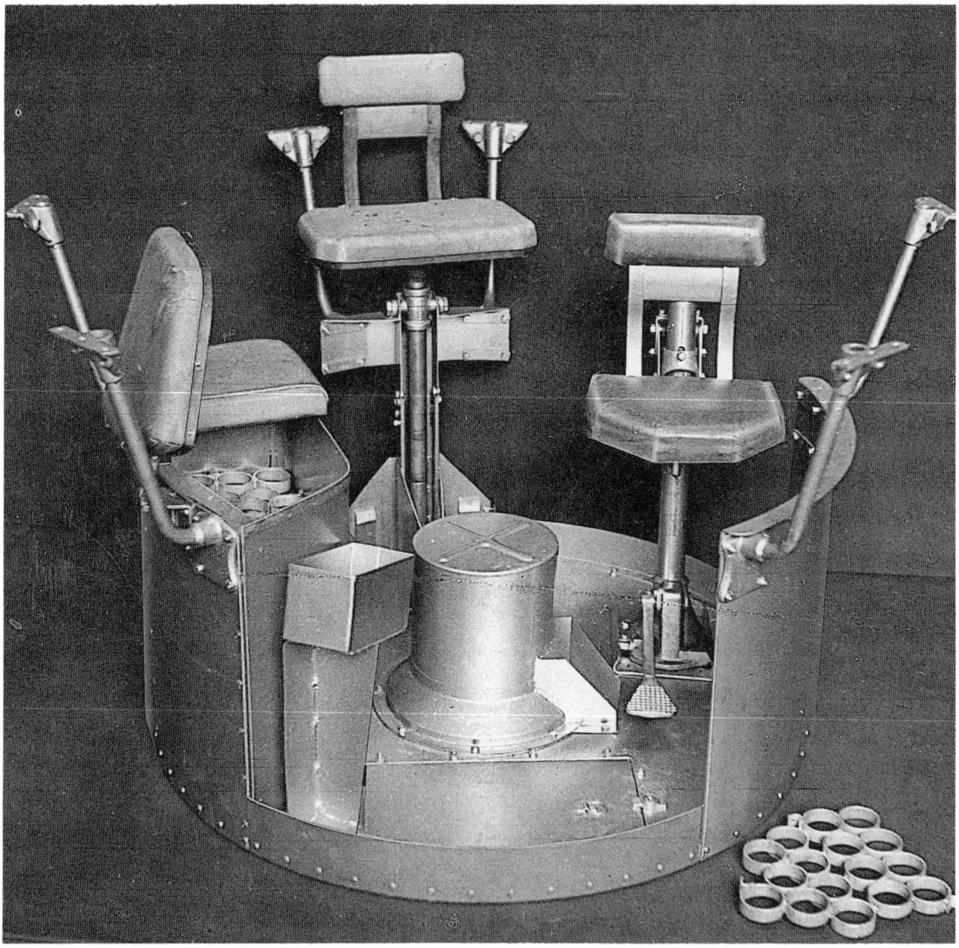

A Jensen-built armoured car.

The Jen-Tug

In 1939, a prototype was built of a new type of commercial vehicle. This was to become known, after the war, as the Jen-Tug. The man responsible for the idea of the Jen-Tug was General Works Manager, Colin Reikie. Reikie's idea was to produce a vehicle that could perform work comparable to that of a single horse drawn vehicle. We may think nowadays that a motor vehicle is a more practical alternative to one that is horse-drawn, but in those pre-war and early post-war years there were still a very large number of horse-drawn vehicles being used. The use of the horse, however, was rapidly succumbing to mechanisation on account of its slower speed, limited radius of operation, its responsibility for traffic congestion, difficulties associated with stabling labour, the ever-increasing cost of fodder and the fact that horse-keeping and driving was becoming less appealing (from a labour point of view) than driving a motor vehicle. The main advantage of the horse was a low initial capital outlay, little depreciation and manoeuvrability in limited and congested space.

These advantages of the horse drawn vehicle were considered very carefully by Reikie and he designed the Jen-Tug to be capable of attaining above the maximum legal speed, a turning circle little more than that of its own length with one full turn of the steering wheel, and even less than its length with more steering applied, a much wider range of operation, and a much quicker turnaround at the loading dock. To keep the labour force happy, much thought was given to the comfort and full weather protection for the driver coupled with easy entry and exit from the cab and visibility and ease of operation.

The prototype was in continuous service throughout the war and by 1946 had completed more than 50,000 miles, which Jensen reckoned was more like 100,000 miles in a normal vehicle, due to the wheel size and very low overall gearing. After some more development the Tug was ready for production

The ubiquitous Jen-Tug in various liveries.

towards the end of 1946. It was made available with fourteen different trailers which could be used for a variety of purposes. These included a simple flat-bed trailer, a light alloy box-body with alloy roller shutter, a tipping chassis, ready to receive the customer's specification of body, a refuse collection body and a long-wheelbase 18 foot platform trailer. If the customer had a desire for a different configuration to the fourteen standard specification bodies, then Jensen would submit designs and quotations to meet operators' individual requirements.

This first design of Jen-Tug was powered by the 10 hp Ford petrol engine which developed 30.1 bhp from its 1172 cc. More important in this application was the engine's torque figure, which in this instance was 46.4 lb/ft at 2400 rpm. This torque figure was perfectly respectable in a light car application, but in practice, in the Jen-Tug, was found to be slightly less than ideal. The complete power unit and transmission (a Ford three forward speed unit) was mounted on a sub-frame which made it possible to remove the whole unit, from radiator to rear axle, quite simply and quickly, by taking out a bolt in the Silentbloc sub-frame mounting, disconnecting the engine and gearbox controls, fuel connection and engine wiring. The sub-frame, which was manufactured from 3 inch pressed steel channel section, was anchored to the main frame by just this one single though substantial Silentbloc mount. The main tractor frame itself was also made from pressed steel channel, this time of 5 inch section.

Semi-elliptic springs were used at the front of the Tug, mounted with plastic bushed pins at the front and a sliding mounting at the rear. Brakes on both tractor and trailer were by Girling, utilizing 11 inch drums. As the braking on a semi-trailer vehicle requires maximum braking effect on the trailer wheels, the trailer drum brakes were of the more efficient twin leading-shoe type, the tractor having the more normal leading and trailing shoes. The brake pedal controlled the tractor brakes hydraulically, with a mechanical linkage to the trailer brakes. The mechanical connection of the trailer brakes was made automatically when the tractor and trailer were coupled together. At the front of the trailer, within an easy arm's length of the seated driver, was a small hand wheel, which when turned would apply or release the trailer brakes when coupling or uncoupling the trailer.

In the construction of the cab of very early models, a certain amount of timber was used, but once supplies started to become more easily obtainable, light alloy was used for panelling and sheet metal work. The cab was designed for ease of use and ease of access. The floor was just 1 ft 9 in above ground level, the seat back-rest was adjustable and the gear lever was mounted on the steering column, just below the steering wheel.

The whole concept of the Jen-Tug was an example of Jensen's ingenuity, but the coupling between tractor and trailer would only serve to emphasize this. The trailer turntable incorporated two non-retracting vertical arms with wheels at the lower end to enable the trailer to be manoeuvred when detached from the tractor. The coupling on the tractor had a single inclined ramp, with deep flanged guide wheels on the trailer. When the flanged-wheel shaft enters the yokes on the trailer coupling, two horizontally disposed hooks envelop it and hold it securely in position. In order to reduce rattle, movement and wear, buffer springs were built into the coupling to keep the relative components in tension.

The Jen-Tug in its many forms proved to be highly successful and profitable, but the Jensen brothers were continually thinking of ways to improve their products and to this end, a Mk 2 Jen-Tug was released towards the end of 1951. It had many improvements and effectively cured any minor criticisms of the earlier vehicles plus gave better performance all round. The Mk 2's carrying capacity was increased from two to three tons. This was achieved mainly by changing the engine to the more modern and powerful Austin A40 unit, but there were many other details involved. The A40 engine came with its four-speed synchromesh gearbox, and had a cubic capacity of 1200 cc developing 40 bhp at 4300 rpm, and, more importantly, 59 lb.ft of torque at 2200 rpm. The engine was fitted with a Lucas distributor governor, restricting engine speed to 4000 rpm. An indirect advantage of using this engine was that the cooling system employed a belt driven water-pump, which was a vast improvement on the Ford engine with its thermo-syphon circulation system. To increase weight and therefore traction on the rear driving wheels, the engine/gearbox unit was moved further back in its subframe. In place of the conventional prop-shaft and universal joints there was a Metalastik trailing link coupling joining the gearbox output shaft to the drive flange on the rear axle. The battery was also repositioned to a new mounting over the gearbox also to improve weight distribution over the rear axle. With larger low-pressure tyres on the driving wheels these improvements made a great difference to the traction and gave the Jen-Tug Mk 2 its greater load capacity.

Jen-Tugs were exported in quantity; this consignment is destined for Africa.

Because the power unit had been moved back, the radiator was repositioned to provide more space between it and the fuel tank. A four-bladed fan was fitted, but two of the blades were readily detachable for use in cooler weather. Another Mk 2 modification was to extend the inlet of the oil-bath air cleaner to a position at the top of the cab. This was in answer to some customers' worries about dust-laden air between the rear wheels being ingested by the engine. The Jensen factory had found difficulty after the war in getting enough supplies of aluminium alloy. They were using it for the Jen-Tug, the JNSN commercial vehicles and the bodywork of their post-war range of cars. So, to leave them with more supply for the other products, and also to keep the cost of the Tug down, the cab of the Mk 2 was built with steel panels. Additional strength was provided by employing gusset plates on the top and lower front corner panels and a bracing plate between the door and rear corner pillars and wheel arches. The engine cover was highly strengthened purely because drivers had been using it as a loading platform and the original design was getting squashed! So instead of the modern idea of a sticker warning operators not to put any weights on the cover, the Jensen redesign made it a very suitable loading platform. Another example of the thought put into the design and improvements concerned trailer lighting. Although the Tug's standard electrical equipment was 12 volt, in the circumstances of the times it was likely that the tug would have to be coupled to a trailer having 6 volt lighting. To overcome this a resistance was included in the circuit to the trailer which would reduce the voltage if necessary.

The Jen-Tug was a remarkable little vehicle that was a successful profit-maker for Jensen Motors in the lean post-war years. Many were sold in the UK but the Tug was also an important product in Jensen's export profits, remembering that all manufacturers were strongly encouraged by the labour government of the day to 'export or die'.

The purchase price of a Jen-Tug Mk 2 tractor unit in April 1953 was £575 plus £92/4/7d purchase tax. The standard thirteen foot platform trailer was priced at £185, the refuse collection body, £495, and the thirteen foot light alloy container body, £332.

The Post-War JNSN Range

After the war had ended, the three JNSNs that had been built for Reynolds, being in continuous service throughout the conflict, had clocked up over 500,000 miles between them. This experience prompted Jensen to offer a standard range of the JNSN Lightweight Diesel Commercial Vehicle, the new vehicle having an unladen weight of 58 cwt and being capable of carrying bulk capacity loads of up to six tons at the permitted speed of 30 mph. It still had an exceptional loading area, this time 23 ft long by 7 ft wide. Jensen stated, in their brochure published late in 1946: 'The bulk capacity load carrier which we now offer to commercial users is a 'thoroughbred' in every sense of the word. It has many exclusive features, the components have been carefully chosen, and in many instances are manufactured to our own designs'.

The newly designed chassis, again a basic chassis/body structure, was built from I-section members of 14-gauge alloy, 16 in deep, riveted top and bottom to flanges of 2 inch alloy angle section. Five cross-members of similar construction were riveted to the side members. Angle section strips, again of aluminium alloy, were riveted to the top flanges of the side and cross members, forming diagonals. Additional strengthening plates were riveted to the frame at the rear spring mounting points. This basic chassis was very light, and even with its riveted construction, experience had shown that it was also immensely strong and durable.

The standard engine was now the well-tried Perkins P6 Aeroflow six-cylinder, developing 70 bhp at 2200 rpm. A British Moss five-speed gearbox and back axle were linked by a three-piece propeller shaft which employed one Layrub and two Hardy Spicer couplings. In the *Commercial Motor* of 19 September 1947 was published details of patent no 588,948, covering the radiator, engine, exhaust, clutch and gearbox unit. The reason for the patent was the system of removing the above in a single unit. If, in service, a replacement engine was required, the front radiator grill panel could be

The JNSN brochure.

removed in about 30 seconds by removing twelve half-turn-release screws, and the complete engine/gearbox unit could then be disconnected and withdrawn in the space of thirty minutes. A replacement unit, always held in stock by Jensen Distributors, could be fitted and connected in about two hours, therefore the vehicle would be off the road for less than three hours. For ease of servicing, the fuel and oil filters were easily accessible by removing the radiator grille panel. Also, to prolong the period between servicing, a Tecalemit pressure-controlled lubricator, actuated by clutch pedal movement, supplied oil to each lubrication point on the chassis. As with their passenger cars, Jensen built in the very latest specification of auxiliary equipment. When many passenger cars were still using mechanical (cable) operated brakes, the JNSN had hydraulic Girling brakes, with 16 inch drums and twin leading shoes, an advanced system for any commercial vehicle. The lighting system was C.A.V. Deluxe, with a split-reflector head-lamp dipping system. The electrical system was 12 volt, with a 120 amp/hour battery and a Lucas 140 watt dynamo. The equipment included electric windscreen wipers (many still used the vacuum system, which meant that the wiper action slowed down as the vehicle speed increased!), a full kit of tools, two driving mirrors, trafficators and a vertically and horizontally adjustable driving seat. The two standard body styles were the usual platform lorry and a Luton pantechnicon which had an enclosed cubic capacity of 1690 cubic feet. Jensen, however, were only too willing to discuss the design of any other type of body that a customer might require.

After the war the business expanded. This led to a second factory being

The unique character of the all-aluminium alloy JNSN chassis can be seen clearly in this photograph.

commissioned in Stoke-on-Trent in 1947, where most of the commercial vehicle work was carried out. In 1951 most of this work was transferred to larger premises at Kingswinford, and then in 1956, the Kelvin Way factory on the Lyttleton Hall Industrial Estate was opened. There was a short period when all these factories were operating simultaneously, but in the late fifties, with less commercial vehicles being produced, the other factories were closed down, the entire operation being then carried out at Kelvin Way.

A removals pantechnicon body on the JNSN chassis.

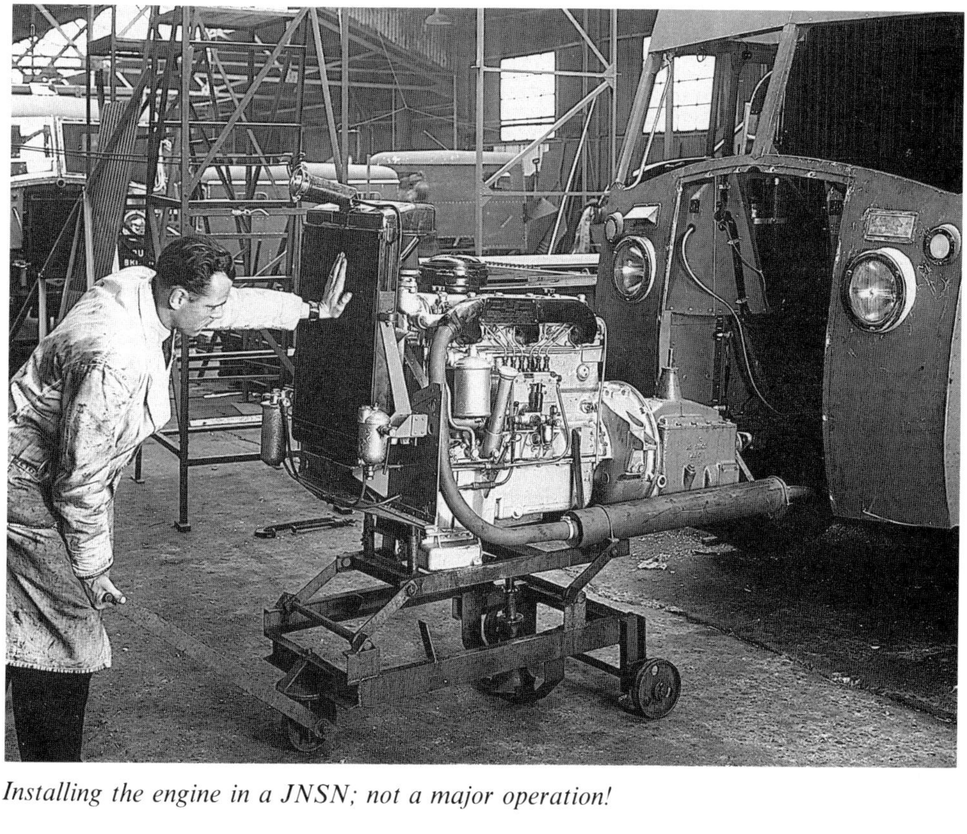

Installing the engine in a JNSN; not a major operation!

The front entrance of a Jensen-built JNSN coach.

A coach body built by Reading & Co. Ltd of Portsmouth on a lightweight JNSN chassis.

The Tempo 25 cwt Hydraulic Elevator Truck

In 1958, Jensen introduced the technically innovative Tempo 1500. Like the Jen-Tug before it, the Tempo was designed to be a small commercial load-carrier, with ease of operation, manoeuvrability and convenience being the key notes. The original design had been German, but the version that Jensen produced under licence had many improvements over the original.

The novel aspect of the Tempo was its hydraulically lowered carrying platform. In their brochure, Jensen stated: 'In industry or agriculture alike the Jensen 25 cwt Elevator Truck with its infinitely variable loading platform height, has unlimited applications. Loading and off-loading at different levels no longer present any difficulty and the necessity for the construction of loading docks and ramps is abolished. Powered by the vehicle engine and operated by a single simple control the elevator truck allows one man to carry out operations normally calling for two men *and* two appliances.'

Mounted on a specially designed and robust tubular chassis, the Tempo had front wheel drive, four wheel independent suspension and offered 50 sq ft of clear load space. The loading platform could be adjusted to any height between ground level and 4 ft 3 in, and was capable of handling payloads with a weight of just over one ton. The engine was the tried and tested BMC B-series 1489 cc four cylinder unit developing 52 bhp at 4000 rpm and 72 lb/ft of torque. It was coupled to a German ZF four-speed gear box, which was integral with the final drive. The gear box had synchromesh on all four forward speeds. The Tempo had a length of 19 ft on a nine ft 10 in wheelbase.

In 1959 Jensen were awarded a contract to build bodies for Austin's four-wheel-drive Gypsy, and Richard and Alan Jensen both assumed that this would be profitable and long term. This was not to be, however, as the Gypsy did not sell as Austin had expected it to. The Land-Rover was the undisputed market leader. The contract came to an end in 1962.

Mounted on a specially designed and robust tubular chassis having front wheel drive and independent suspension on all wheels, the Jensen Tempo offered some 50 sq ft of clear loading space.

The Austin Gypsy contract did not last as long as Jensen had hoped.

4

The Post-war Years

ON 30 AUGUST 1946, *Autocar* magazine published a description of an entirely new 4-litre Jensen. The brochure that Jensen had had printed proclaimed the car as 'The Jensen Four Litre Straight Eight', but the car was to become known as the 'PW' model, for reasons that should be obvious.

The *new* car was not really entirely new, however, because it had a chassis based on the pre-war HC type. Richard and Alan Jensen, while keeping their factory busy throughout the war years had nevertheless been planning ahead whenever they had the opportunity. Therefore the PW model was intended to be simply a stepping stone to the firm's intended post-war activities.

Autocar was very interested in this chassis, outlining the new technique in construction:

> One of the interesting features of the side members is that they are not built up from the usual channel sections with sides welded on to form a box, but are cut out to shape from four flat steel strips, which are set in a jig and electrically arc welded along the edges from end to end.
>
> The advantages of this fabricated method of construction are that expensive dies are not needed, whilst the scope for variation in shape to suit design is considerably increased. At the front end the side members are braced together by a stout cross-tube, welded in on both sides of each box section. Below the cross-tube is a detachable sub-assembly which provides the base for the independent front suspension linkage. This sub-assembly consists of two cross-members, of inverted channel section, some distance apart. Their ends are bolted on below the frame side-members. They are joined together by a centrally placed fore-and-aft member of channel section, which is welded in place, reinforced wherever necessary, and which forms a strut between the points of attachment of the suspension lower wishbones.

Stiff though it was, the frame was further reinforced by welding the flat steel floor-pan into place on the chassis, which was a tried and tested Jensen method.

The interest in this new car tended to centre not on this new chassis construction, but on a completely new engine designed for the car by Henry Meadows Ltd, of Fallings Park, Wolverhampton, a firm, with a long and enviable reputation for very reliable high-speed engines.

The 1948 PW Continental Saloon.

Meadows had designed a very advanced engine; it was again a straight eight-cylinder (like the pre-war Nash), but much of its construction was of aluminium alloy. It was a 'square' engine design, with the bore and stroke measuring 85 mm. It was one of the first post-war engines to be announced which had taken into account the new British taxation formula. It really was an up-to-the-minute design.

The specification of this engine included a crankshaft mounted on nine steel-backed bearings. The timing gear was arranged, unusually, at the *back* of the cylinder-block, reducing crankshaft backlash. At the front end of the shaft was a torsional harmonic vibration damper of the rubber-mounted type. Wet-liners formed the cylinder barrels, these being made of a nickel-copper-iron alloy, being pressed into the aluminium cylinder block casting. To minimise the possibility of distortion, the engine was designed with two cylinder-heads, each covering four cylinders. The valve seat inserts were made of high expansion steel, the valve springs being of a compound specification. The high position of the camshaft ensured short and light push-rods, which operated one of the early hydraulic tappet arrangements, being primed by full oil pressure.

The air/petrol mixture was provided by two of the early SU horizontal carburettors, which incorporated silencers within the filtration system. These carburettors were fed by a mechanical AC fuel pump, which was situated at the front end of the engine, this position chosen because the pump was being cooled by the radiator cooling fan.

The capacity of this unusual engine was 3860 cc and it developed 130 bhp at 4300 rpm from a compression ratio of 6.25:1, figures which show that it was relatively unstressed at this early stage and obviously had plenty of potential for higher outputs at a later date. Sadly, there wasn't to be a later date for the Meadows engine. During testing, there had been some problems with crankshaft vibrations at high speeds, and although both Henry Meadows Ltd and Jensen tried to overcome this, they never achieved the smoothness and refinement that Richard and Alan Jensen were requiring. So, very late on in the PWs development (indeed after *Autocar* had published their new model description), the Jensen brothers were faced with the daunting task of finding another suitable engine. The model, complete with Meadows engine, had been introduced to the public at the British Motor Industry's Jubilee Cavalcade in July 1946, *Autocar* had published their report in August and Jensen had commissioned a four-page brochure giving comprehensive technical specifications including a cut-away drawing taken from the *Autocar* article. Luckily, there were still a few of the Nash straight eight-cylinder engines left over from the pre-war models, and to enable prompt delivery of the first four PWs (for which orders had been placed), these engines were used. This did not solve the problem, however, and another engine had to be found to power future PW models.

The replacement engine presented itself almost providentially some seven months later. Richard Jensen was travelling to London with his five-year old son, Martin. Martin – interested, of course, in motor cars – suddenly exclaimed

A Jensen PW Saloon during construction, showing aluminium panelwork over the ash frame.

The fascia of the PW model.

to his father that he had spotted another Jensen! Richard turned to look at the parked car and realised that it looked very much like a PW – but it wasn't. Closer investigation showed that it was an Austin, an Austin Sheerline. Richard remembered that when his PW was on show at the Jubilee Cavalcade, Leonard Lord, the Managing Director of the Austin Motor Company, and a group of colleagues, had showed rather a lot of interest. Richard assumed that Lord and his team must have copied his design, then in its prototype stage, hoping to get it into production before the Jensen product.

Understandably, Richard Jensen was rather put out, and he immediately arranged a meeting with Leonard Lord. When Jensen put forth the opinion that he would soon be out of business if Lord was selling a product that *looked* the same, but at a much reduced cost, Lord tried to appease him by offering to supply Jensens with their Sheerline 4-litre six-cylinder engine. Lord knew of the difficulty that Jensen were having finding a suitable engine for the PW model, and that this was effectively stopping full production going ahead. Richard Jensen could do nothing but accept, because the new engine would put him back in business, and he knew himself that the Sheerline would never really be a threat to a car the calibre of the PW.

As it turned out, the Sheerline engine was a very reliable, modern, though not innovative, and reasonably powerful design. The Austin unit was almost the same cubic capacity (Meadows, 3860 cc; Austin, 3993 cc), and it developed the same power of 130 bhp at 4000 rpm. One slight problem remained though: the very expensively printed brochures detailing the new 'Jensen Four Litre Straight Eight'. Nowadays this would be a triviality, but in 1947, with all the other problems that the Jensen management had to consider, it was something of a headache! A simple solution was found: the same brochure was kept.

However, these brochures were modified, by block-printing black over the words 'Straight Eight' thus leaving the legend, 'The Jensen Four-Litre'. On page two, the panel of specifications (including the Meadows engine specification) was covered with a stick-on panel outlining the revised specifications of the Austin engine and the prices: Chassis only, £1300; 4-door Saloon, £1826 (plus tax); four-door convertible, £2180 (plus tax). These prices actually represented a reduction of £100, due to the cheaper Austin engine. The cut-away drawing of the PW was unchanged though, so prospective customers must have been bemused to read a brochure outlining the 4-litre six cylinder Jensen, and seeing a drawing of what was obviously an eight-cylinder engine.

At last the PW was in production, and the quality of construction was to the usual Jensen high standard. The frame of the bodywork was constructed partly of steel and partly of the more usual timber. The panelwork was aluminium alloy. The interior was quite roomy, capable of carrying six people in comfort, and in spite of the low body line, there was still plenty of headroom, due to the floor panel being part of the chassis, and not mounted above it. The seating was plush, Jensen offering separate front seats or a single bench type. In place of the more usual wood or bakelite window edge capping there was a narrow chrome-plated strip which gave a more finished appearance. The door hinges were concealed, and the front windscreen had a control to open it in the top central rail of the dashboard. The polished walnut fascia had a lockable glovebox on the extreme left-hand side, the engine revolution counter being on the extreme right. On the central fascia panel, the speedometer (marked both in miles-per-hour and kilometres-per-hour) was on the left, with another large dial incorporating four supplementary gauges, on the left. The spare wheel had been moved to the side of the left-hand front wing which gave a useful 20 cubic feet luggage boot.

The PW range (which included a unique *four-door* convertible) was important in the story of Jensen because it was their first post-war model, and gave them a firm footing for their plans for the future. Due to their eventual choice of engine it also gave them a valuable working relationship with the Austin Motor Company, which was to prove very useful in years to come.

A New Recruit into Jensen's Drawing Office

During a conversation with an old acquaintance, Bill Handley, Richard Jensen was told of a friend of Handley's who had just returned to Wolseley Motors Ltd after his war service and was dissatisified with the way the Wolseley management had changed in his absence. Handley explained to Richard that his friend was an exceedingly skilled and experienced designer, and knowing Richard's plans for the future, put it to him that this man could be a valuable asset to Jensen's drawing office. This man was Eric Neale.

Eric Neale was born one year after Richard Jensen, on the 26 September, 1910, in Halesowen, Worcestershire. His father had been in the timber industry since the age of 12 and joined Austins at Longbridge in 1916. This new career was interrupted, however, by his being called up for active service in the Royal Flying Corps. He returned to Longbridge three years later and resumed work, becoming eventually Superintendent of Timber Processing and Production.

Eric, the eldest of six children, had won a scholarship to Halesowen

Grammar School and after five years gained a good matriculation in July 1927. He thus left school and asked his father if he could try to get him a job in the up-and-coming motor body industry. One of his father's colleagues spoke to the management of Mulliners in Birmingham who went on to accept Eric as an apprentice designer, under the care and tutorage of James Wignal. This was in August 1927, just before Eric's seventeenth birthday.

Jimmie Wignal (his uncle was works manager at Gurney-Nutting, the coachbuilders), was a first class designer and was the finest possible teacher that the young Eric Neale could have had, introducing him to pencil and brush-work for custom body sketches for clients all over Britain and the Continent. He gained experience in helping to design bodies for all types of chassis including Rolls-Royce, Minerva, Daimler, Panhard-Levassor, Stutz and Packard. There was also the designing of quantity-produced bodies like the 16 hp Austin two-seater, War Office Austin Sevens and Clyno saloons. Wignal would produce full-size drawings showing all the shapes and timber structures from which expert pattern-makers would make all the jigs and bucks for the requirements of the saw-mill and body shop.

Eric Neale still has fond memories of these early days at Mulliners: 'Gradually I acquired a little knowledge, and Jim told me of the Institute of British Coachwork and Automobile Manufacturers, which was to play a great part in my life from then to the present day. He encouraged me to enter one of their design competitions which he himself was entering, which required a $^1/_{16}$ scale coloured design (side view and plan) of any body type on any chassis.

'There were two prizes on offer, and Jim's entry came second. My entry, apparently, was considered worthy enough for the judges to award a special third prize. Jim and I were both delighted.'

Talking to many of the skilled pattern and jig makers employed at Mulliners, Eric realised that they all had considerable experience of different working practices at different coachbuilders. He became concerned that he should get out and about and gain some more experience himself. For that reason, he left Mulliners in 1929, and joined Holbrook Bodies Ltd in Coventry. Holbrooks were making bodies for Alvis, Triumph and Armstrong-Siddeley. After less than two years, however, Eric left and joined the Singer Motor Company, Birmingham, as a body designer/draughtsman.

After designing the Singer 9 hp Saloon, Eric was asked to do a 9 hp four-seater sports. His designs started to excite a few people and Singer's Managing Director, W.E. Bullock, asked his son, 'Young' Bill, to move the body-drawing office to Coventry for closer contact with the chassis and engine and gearbox designers. The next body design was the 'Le Mans' two-seater, at first 9 hp and then with the larger $1^1/_2$-litre engine.

Eric Neale continues, 'Chief body draughtsman at that time was Ted Skelcher, my closest friend. Following a dispute with W.E. Bullock, he went for a meeting with the Daimler management. On his return he informed us that they were engaging him to set up and run a new body drawing office, but were in need of an artist/designer. Would I go and see them? I then met Laurence Pomeroy Senior, Daimler Engineering Director and his right-hand man, J. Simpson. After a chat with them I accepted their offer.'

Over the next two years Neale's design projects included the 18 hp Lanchester Saloon, 15 hp Daimler Saloon and BSA 12 hp Saloon, and

Eric Neale.

embraced radiator shell design for all models, with the introduction of the first curved Daimler shells. The Daimler aim for silence in chassis/body design was paramount, and was largely accomplished. Eric remembers, 'Towards the end of 1936, at the time of the impending abdication of the then Prince of Wales, I had gradually concluded that it was time to get close aquaintance with modern motor body production processes and so joined the West Efficiency Department at Austin's, which planned the body build from the handling of the sheet metal right through to the painting, trimming and finishing, ready for the mounting operation in the South Works.

'This involved me in the design of sub-assembly and track jigs with specialised spot and arc-welding equipment, time and motion study, including cycle times tied to daily track production figures. I had to draw the covered track layout with all stations detailed both in plan layout and perspective. After a little over a year I felt that my design outlook now had a fairly useful back-up, and, hearing of the requirement for a body draughtsman, I was accepted by Wolseley at Washwood Heath. This was early 1938, and in a very short time Wolseley's managing director, Miles Thomas, was taking my designs down to William Morris himself, at Oxford, for approval.

'However, after drawing the new 12 hp Wolseley Saloon and Coupé, the realisation of impending hostilities changed our work: we were now designing ambulances, army trucks, etc. Even depth-charge pistols came within our orbit.'

Miles Thomas had been a Wing Commander in the Middle East in the First World War, but although he tried hard to keep Eric Neale, after a little difficulty over the question of whether Eric's occupation was "reserved" or not, he finally had to recommend Eric for service. Eric Neale joined the Royal Air Force in August 1940. After service in Britain, Egypt, the Lebanon and Italy, he returned to England in November 1944 and was demobilised at the end of November 1945. He married two weeks later.

Eric returned to Wolseleys at Washwood Heath, it being a legal requirement that demobbed servicemen might return to their former employ if they so wished. He received a rather cold welcome, however, from the Chief Engineer, a Dutchman, Marie Van Eugen, who informed him that he could not expect the same seniority or remuneration as the staff that had remained in the drawing office. During the war, Miles Thomas had moved to Oxford and Eric Neale felt that changes had been made, and also that as the factory was just beginning to start thinking of peacetime motor vehicle production, he had not rejoined the job that he had left.

'My old friend Bill Handley told Richard Jensen about my activities, and this culminated in meeting him one evening in May 1946 at the Carters Green factory when everyone else had gone home. Just the two of us toured the plant and Richard told me of his ambitions. He made me an offer, and I accepted. I joined him a fortnight later for a close association that would last for the next twenty years.'

Eric Neale seemed to share Richard and Alan Jensen's views on car design and they immediately settled into a steady and fruitful working relationship.

The first Jensen Interceptor, and the Austin A40 Sports

When Richard Jensen had sorted out the problem of the PW's power unit, intending now to use the Austin engine, Eric Neale remarked, 'That's fine, but why don't Austin consider introducing a sports car? There hasn't been one in their range since the pre-war Sevens.'

The idea was to stay in Eric's mind, but was not to come to fruition until Richard Jensen's own ideas on the subject matured. He had for some time felt that he should be producing a fast, long-distance sports tourer, which the PW clearly was not. Richard had the idea of designing a car that used a readily available chassis, as well as readily available power-train, which would enable

A series of shots showing the features of the Interceptor Hard-top.

production and development to be speeded up. As he had already secured a supply of engines from Austin, Richard again approached Leonard Lord with a view to Austin's supplying their A70 chassis. Lord agreed, but with one condition.

Richard returned and headed straight to the drawing office to confront Eric Neale, who was his Body Design and Development Engineer. He had a slightly perplexed look on his face.

'What's the matter?' asked Eric, 'Won't Austin supply the parts?'

'Yes, they *will* supply the parts,' replied Richard Jensen, 'but they also

Left and above: *the interior of the Jensen Interceptor.*

In July 1954 Mr Eigil Jensen of Los Angeles takes delivery of the latest Interceptor from Alan and Richard Jensen.

want us to design and build a prototype sports car, based on an Austin chassis and Austin mechanicals!'

Both Richard and Eric realised the value of such a contract for Jensen Motors Ltd. It would be a valuable boost to their cash-flow, remembering the fact that Jensen Motors at that time were making their money from body manufacture, not from their own specialist motor cars. Eric submitted quite a few designs for this Austin-based sports car to Longbridge, but his main efforts were concentrated on developing Richard Jensen's sports tourer and the Austin sports car, as 'an Austin and a Jensen from the same stable'. The idea was to make common quite a few of the body jigs and parts, with the amount of design work involved being reduced. As luck would have it, it was this design (based on the Austin A40) that Leonard Lord was impressed with, and he thus commissioned Jensen to build the bodies for this new car, which was to be called the Austin A40 Sports.

Another view of Eigil Jensen's Interceptor.

A customer-specified extra chrome side-trim makes this Interceptor Cabriolet very sleek. It was bought by a Mr H. McCalman in 1954.

Early Interceptor showing vent on forward end of bonnet allowing airflow direct to radiator header tank. This feature was discontinued on later cars.

Major Weir takes the girls from the typing pool for a spin . . .

. . . and the resulting cunningly retouched photograph is used as a Jensen publicity shot . . .

The Jensen model was to be called the Interceptor, a name coined by Lord Strathcarron, a close friend of Richard Jensen. Eric Neale explained, 'The A40 Sports and Interceptor design and development was a combined and integrated operation. Before commencing working and presentation drawings, I was so concerned to win a Longbridge order, that I pushed on with the A40 prototype, causing Richard and Alan to fret about the Interceptor's completion in time for the motor show for which it was booked [Earls Court 1949]. To their relief, all the lads involved in the shops pulled the stops out, working through the night to complete in time'.

. . . but one of the unfortunate girls got the "boot"!

So the new Jensen Interceptor was announced in October 1949. Eric Neale had produced a two-door drophead body which was described as a full four-seater; there was a bench seat in the front, the rear seat leg-room being adequate rather than roomy. It was powered by a single carburettor version of the Austin Sheerline engine and could manage a top speed of just under 100

Two views of the Jensen-bodied Austin A90 Atlantic which had been requested by Leonard Lord or George Harriman of Austin in 1951.

mph, driving through the standard Austin four-speed gearbox although overdrive became standard equipment in later versions.

Two models were offered, the cabriolet and the fixed-head. The design of the folding hood on the cabriolet was innovative in that the rear window and rear quarter-lights were moulded from rigid perspex, which swung into wells in the bodywork when the hood was lowered.

The owner of this Interceptor was a South African magistrate who valued his Jensen for reliability and comfort as he travelled to various outlying country courthouses taking his African manservant with him everywhere. Every year he would drive his Jensen up through North Africa to the Mediterranean. The car was shipped across and then the owner would drive the car up through Spain and France to the English Channel. Upon crossing he would take the car up to Jensen's at West Bromwich for its annual service. When the service was completed, the owner headed back home!

Jensen were still offering coach-built bodies for any suitable customer's chassis. This is an Invicta with drop-head coupé bodywork by Jensen.

Rear three-quarter view of the Invicta coupé.

Although Leonard Lord had accepted Eric Neale's proposals for the A40-based sports car, the Austin A40 Sports, when it was unveiled at the London Motor Show the year *after* the Interceptor, was a certain compromise on Neale's original ideas. His original design, totally influenced by the emerging post-war Italian body designs, was to have had a much lower body than the A40, and a fairly high top gear ratio to give effortless fast cruising. This was not to be, however, for Austin said that the ground clearance would not be high enough for motoring in remote areas of the world. As Eric Neale stated, 'This was the period when British manufacturers were attacking Empire markets with type variants having wider tracks, greater ground clearance and tougher suspension to suit veldt, outback and prairie'.

Austin also did not like the high gearing as the first prototype would not climb their local test hill in top gear, so they lowered the axle ratio. One Jensen modification to the chassis that Austin accepted was to the road springs to reduce wheel bump, as the A40 Sports had a very much lighter body than the standard Devon saloon that provided the chassis. Eric Neale went on, 'Hence the high A40 Sports, with which we at West Bromwich could not argue as we so badly needed the order for Body Production – and went on to build 3200 examples, out of a curtailed order of 3500'.

Production began in early 1951. The Austin chassis had cross-bracing added and this was boxed in to give extra rigidity. The interior was designed along very similar lines to the Interceptor, although there was a hood stowage well behind the rear seat back.

The engine had been modified with a more efficient cylinder head and twin SU carburettors. This lifted the power output from 40 to 50 bhp which

Early drawings of Eric Neale's, illustrating his theme of an Austin and a Jensen from the same stable.

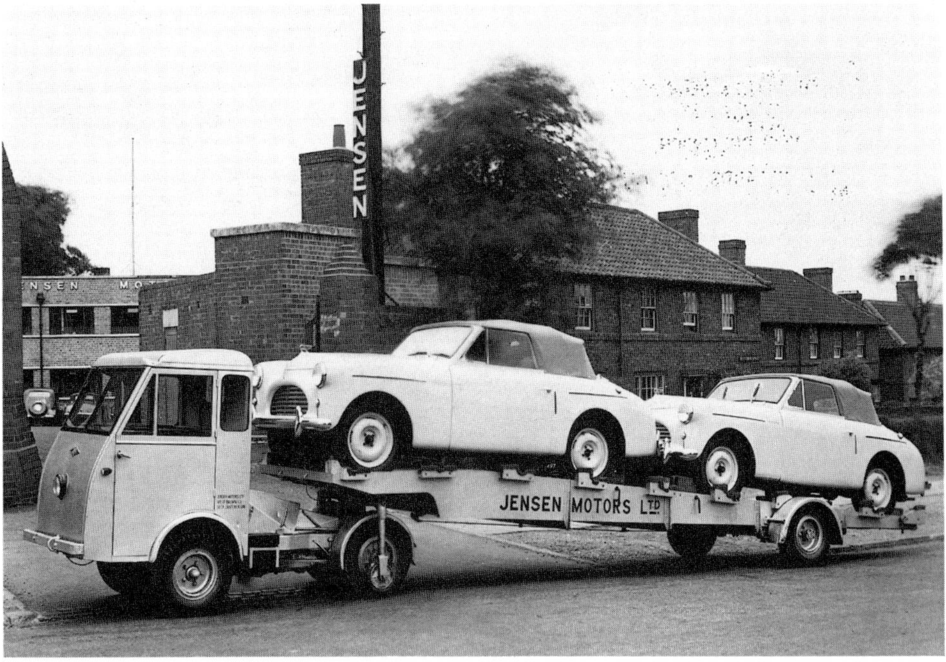

The Jen-Tug carrying two Austin A40 Sports.

increased the top speed and acceleration of the car, *The Motor* recording a 0–60 mph time of 25.6 seconds. They stated that this was a figure 45 per cent better than that of the original Austin Saloon. The motoring press in both Britain and the United States gave the little car a warm reception, but it never actually sold in very large quantities. Austin had assumed that as the car provided economical open-air motoring for four people, it should sell readily in the US. But the American idea of room for four people was not to echo Austin's, and they were not too worried about fuel economy either. Of the 2573 A40 Sports exported, only 643 of them found their way into American showrooms. It was withdrawn from production in 1953.

An early drawing of the prototype sports car Eric Neale styled for Leonard Lord in 1952. It bears a striking resemblance to the MGA introduced in 1954.

Another of Eric Neale's ideas for the Austin-based sports car.

This car was designed around Austin mechanicals and certain other components.

In 1952, Austin and Morris merged and formed the new British Motor Corporation. There was still a personal rivalry between Austin's Leonard Lord and Morris's Lord Nuffield and neither could agree on determining BMC's future sports car policy. So Nuffield asked MG to submit some designs, and these eventually became the MGA. Lord again approached Jensen Motors Ltd and asked them to design an entirely new sports car, based on current Austin

This is the sports car that Eric designed for the 1952 Motor Show, but due to shortage of certain components the car was not ready for display.

mechanical components. Eric Neale subsequently submitted a design based on a new cruciform chassis, with very stylish open two-seater bodywork. The car was to be ready for the London Motor Show in October, but was not completed in time, due to late delivery of some electrical parts from Lucas and brake parts from Automotive Products.

Donald Healey has also been working on a new sports car which was also based on Austin mechanicals, the engine being the 2.6-litre A90 unit. This car, the Healey 100, was ready just in time for Earls Court, and was brought in just as the stands were being set up.

This is the same car years later with added hard-top and restyled front end.

Rear view of later modifications.

The original Interceptor Cabriolet.

Leonard Lord saw this new Healey and decided that it was just the sports car Austin were looking for. He immediately got in touch with Donald Healey and a deal was struck. Austin would manufacture and market the car, and it would become known as the Austin-Healey 100. A new badge was produced overnight by Wilmot-Breedon and rushed to Earls Court to be fitted to the new car before the show's official opening.

Eric Neale had been doing his usual early reconnaissance and learned of BMC's acquisition at first hand. He also discovered that the car was to be built at Tickfords and that production would be in the region of 40 cars per week. Eric continues, 'I immediately sought Richard Jensen, gave him this news, and knowing he had arranged to meet Leonard Lord on the Saturday, I asked him to suggest that Jensen Motors would produce 150 a week in primer! It was obvious to me that most people were ignorant of the car's sales potential'.

The meeting between Richard Jensen and Leonard Lord was held at Jensen's show office at Earls Court. When it was over Richard explained to Eric Neale that Lord wanted to see the Jensen prototype sports car, as an example of their work, before he finally decided to award them the Healey contract. Eric went back to West Bromwich, obtained the undelivered parts himself and completed the car before the end of the following week. When Lord saw it, he was very impressed, and straight away confirmed the Austin-Healey body-building contract with Jensens. They then took over the full size drawings from Healey at Warwick, and immediately set about designing their own layouts from which they produced the 25 prototypes. From this point, all subsequent styling and body engineering was handled by Jensen, until the car ceased production in 1966.

The prototype Jensen sports was sent back to West Bromwich and over the years was used for styling experiments by Eric Neale and other members of the drawing office. First a hard-top was added, which made the car look a little like the MGA coupé, or the fixedhead XK120. In later years the centre section between the front wings was completely revised, removing the original Austin 7 grille and replacing it with a more traditional radiator shell bearing a Jensen badge.

One thing was certain though: the Austin-Healey body-building contract had provided Jensen with the financial resources to start developing an all-new Grand Touring car as a successor to the Interceptor. So for the all-important London Motor Show in 1953, Jensen had a new model of their own to show. It was called, simply, the 541.

5

The 541 Series

THE NEW CAR project was formed in early February 1953. Richard Jensen had approached Eric Neale, Body Design and Development Engineer, and Colin Reikie, General Works Manager, and asked their opinions on the possibility of producing a new car, smaller than the Interceptor, still being a full four-seater, and having a very high performance. The three discussed a few different ideas, and Eric Neale put forward the idea of a four-seater GT saloon, using low-drag aerodynamic bodwork to complement the power output of Austin's 4-litre engine. During production of the Interceptor and the A40 Sports, one or two trade magazines had reported on the introduction of glass-fibre and polyester resin being used in the USA for one-off motor body parts. A few enquiries to their many suppliers soon provided the new materials and information on current techniques, and experimental work had begun in

One of Eric Neale's early factory publicity drawings of the 541.

The original alloy-bodied Jensen 541 before it was registered for road use.

the Body Development Department. Prototype Interceptor panels had been made and thoroughly tested for strength and the suitability of different painting systems. The tests were a success and the new material was chosen for the bodywork of the new car.

Richard Jensen had decided that they should now build their own chassis frames, as they had decided that the new glass-fibre shell would not contribute much structural stiffness. He decided, then, on a new ladder type frame, comprising very strong tubular side members with boxed or tubular cross-members. Both Reikie and Neale were delighted with this choice of construction, which was to use 5 inch diameter 11-gauge circular drawn tubes as its basis, and Eric Neale, having been involved previously with torsion-testing at Daimler, was 100 per cent behind Richard Jensen's decision.

Although the car was envisaged as a full four-seater, there were no restrictions placed on length or width of the new car, so it was designed from scratch, with a seating mock-up being made with four seats placed on a platform mounted $8^1/2$ inches above the ground, this being considered a suitable ground clearance. The engine/gearbox unit was positioned within this desired ground clearance and the front axle line was placed well forward of the engine to give a 50/50 weight distribution. With the mock-up finalised, its dimensions were transferred to a working quarter-scale drawing, and at this point the position of the back axle was determined. Thus the wheelbase worked out at 105 inches.

The final frame configuration was worked out; the 5 inch diameter side tubes were joined by four cross-members of $2^1/2$ inch diameter, placed with two at the front scuttle area, one above the propeller shaft line and one below, one on top of the wheel arch connecting the rear damper mountings, and one more at the rear above the spring shackles. A square cross-member coincided with the gearbox mounting.

In the experimental build shop (just opposite the drawing office), the chassis was put together. Torsional stiffness was considered paramount because of the glass-fibre body, and the chassis was tested at first with the gearbox-mounting square cross-member welded to the chassis as a complete box-section, with no provision for the gearbox mounting cradle. Torque was applied to the section between the planes of the front and rear axles, the rear being fixed and the front mounted on a central pivot, the resulting deflection being noted. The central box-section was then cut for fitment of the gearbox support cradle and the torsional stiffness test repeated. The cradle was modified and stiffened and tested again. The process was repeated three times until the original torque deflection figure was achieved once again. Satisfied with the strength of the chassis, it was further built up, adding rear wheel arches, boot floor and bulkhead, and transferred to the body shop.

Eric Neale designed his new body directly around the dimensions of the new chassis. Since the war many cars had been designed with radiator grilles with louvres or panels that could be shut or simple radiator blinds that would guard against freezing driving conditions. Because Eric wanted a low-drag clean-shaped front panel the usual flat or V-sectioned grille was not considered. His answer was the horizontally pivoted front intake panel that was to become so much a part of the 541 model. The name for the new car had finally been chosen; at this time quite a few manufacturers were discarding model names and started using figure codes. Eric suggested the designation '531' to Richard, but he reminded Eric that this was the construction title of Cunard's new trans-Atlantic liner, and also that when showing a new car, one always used the following year for dating. Thus 541 for 1954.

For this first prototype, the body was aluminium panelled. With Richard Jensen's intention to show the new car at Earls Court in October, there simply was not time to fabricate the body moulds and then produce the panels in glass-fibre. Eric Neale's full-sized body drawings showed cross-sections and longitudinal sections at every ten inches; these drawings showing the skin lines as well as the structural members. The skin line sections were traced onto transparent paper and these were, in turn, transferred onto ply-wood sheets which were then cut to the skin line form. These sections were interlocked with the longitudinal ones and thus formed a jig on which the aluminium panels were formed.

The suspension and steering layout was based on the Austin A70 components, but followed Jensen's own steering geometry design. The steering layout presented a problem because there were over 150 steering units left over from the PW Saloon, and Richard Jensen did not want to waste them. This system was therefore used instead of the A70's rack and pinion, and there were no objections from Colin Reikie, as he was not fond of rack and pinion steering anyway. Again, there was no time to manufacture new forgings to make the PW's cam and rocker steering unit mate to the A70 suspension, so a set of levers was fabricated from rectangular section 10-gauge sheet which was folded and bent to reproduce exactly the ball joint positions intended for the forgings.

With the introduction of the 541 at the 1953 Motor Show, the Interceptor was still to be kept in production.

Reikie placed two 8½ gallon fuel tanks under the rear seat area, again to help weight distribution. The twin exhaust system would therefore run in the tunnel formed under the propeller shaft between the two petrol tanks. Two silencers (the same two used on the Interceptor's single system) were fitted just under the boot floor, with the two short tail-pipes almost in line with each rear wheel. This configuration was to prove less than ideal as was found out later. It was October, and the car was nearly finished, but there were numerous details to attend to. The car was put on a JNSN lorry and taken to Earls Court. It still had not been driven under its own steam; the brake lines were still not fitted, a temporary handbrake was rigged up to enable the car to be moved about, no battery had been fitted and there were still no external fillers for the twin petrol tanks.

There was immediate interest in the 541 at the Motor Show; from prospective customers as well as other manufacturers, as Jensen had stated clearly that production models were to have bodies built of resin-bonded glass-fibre. Jensen's problem was now how to get the car into production as quickly as possible, and as soon as the car was returned to West Bromwich work began on getting the car into running order. A proper handbrake system was installed, the brake pipes fitted and a battery temporarily fitted. Two weeks later it was taken for its first run. The engine had been taken from an Interceptor that had completed 50,000 miles (a director's car), so there was no need to run it in; testing could begin in earnest right away.

Close-up of the swivelling bonnet-flap on the 541.

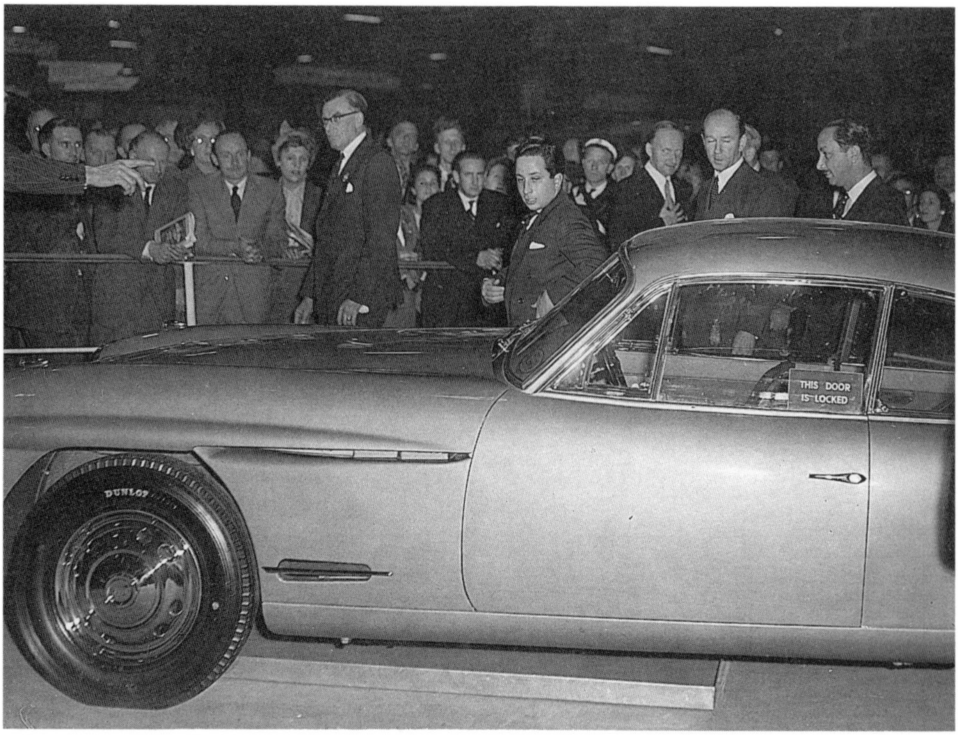

King Feisal of Iraq visits the Jensen stand.

The glass-fibre finishing shop at West Bromwich.

541 Fascia.

A 541 fitted with the wire-wheel option.

The first problem that came to light was the noise; the exhaust was noisy and there was also a bad booming within the bodyshell. Everyone that drove it agreed that it was embarrassingly loud, so a new exhaust system was designed. The original system was thought to be too loud due to the silencers being unsuitable and too far back, resulting in too short tail-pipes. The new system was designed with twin pipes running under the left-hand side of the floor into twin silencers now mounted just below the rear seat pan and thence into two long tail-pipes that ran off to the left to clear the spare wheel. Various different silencers had been tried, differing only in their internals, as the outside dimensions were dictated by the available space. Due to this new configuration the twin under-seat fuel tanks were dispensed with and a single tank designed to fit under the boot floor with a recess at the back to accommodate the front of the spare wheel. At least this rearrangement provided a better home for the battery, and it was placed in a cradle underneath the right-hand rear seat pan. While this work was being done the opportunity was taken to experiment with brake wheel cylinders to try to improve the front/rear braking balance.

A proud customer taking delivery of his 541 from Richard Jensen (on left).

The 541 Saloon at Earls Court in 1954.

The car was now ready for the road and was therefore registered, gaining the number JEA 541. The exhaust silencer was immeasurably improved, and proper long-term road-testing began. The car was still being run with the temporary fabricated steering arms, and the dies for the new forgings were being made. These fabricated arms seemed to be doing the job quite well until one day after Richard Jensen had just returned the car to the experimental shop after a long fast run from London. Later on that afternoon it became necessary to move the back a few yards, so it was pushed. As it moved, both front wheels swung to full toe-in. One of the fabricated arms had sheared through metal fatigue! No further risks were taken and the car stayed in that position for just over a week until the new forged steering arms arrived and were fitted.

Engine Development

When the body had originally been designed it was clear that the downdraught Stromberg carburettor as used on the Interceptor engine was not going to fit under the bonnet line. The 4-litre Austin Princess had previously used triple sidedraught SUs but this set-up was also considered unsuitable as the front and rear carburettors were angled up at 30 degrees although the centre one was horizontal. Reikie and the engineers working on the project had the idea that if they used the Princess centre manifold for all three carburettors, the resulting horizontal configuration would fit under the 541's bonnet. Jensen had to obtain their own supply, because the set-up was not being used by Austin any more.

The triple-carburettor Austin 4-litre engine as fitted to the 541.

The maximum permissible amount was also machined off the cylinder-head to raise the compression ratio. The result of these modifications was almost a 25 per cent increase in power with a little more torque throughout the rev range.

In early 1954 the car was taken over to Longbridge to test it in Austin's wind tunnel, and find out if these engine power increases, mated to Eric Neale's low-drag body, would result in the very high performance and high speed stability that was expected. As it turned out, Eric had designed an aerodynamic masterpiece for, to express it in modern terms, the drag coefficient was just over 0.36 – a figure that is only now being bettered by production motor cars. With the bonnet flap open, because of the resulting drag, the C_D was raised to 0.39, but this was still a very acceptable figure.

The final report on the wind tunnel tests was put together by Austin's D.P. Harris, of their development department. His report, no. 1579/057, dated 21 January 1954, commented on the low wind drag of the 541. 'The wind drag of the Jensen 541 Saloon car has been measured in the wind tunnel,' he began. 'The radiator intake of the car is fitted with a hinged shutter, and tests were carried out with the shutter fully open, and with it closed. In its best form the car's drag coefficient is .00100, a very low figure. It can be seen how remarkable is the effect of opening the radiator intake; although the intake is well situated and of good shape it increases the car's drag by 17 per cent.'

Also shown was a graph of the estimated total resistance of the car at all speeds. It was deduced that in standard form, the maximum speed of the 541 would be 122 mph. This turned out to be slightly optimistic, most production examples attaining 115 – 117 mph. Mr Harris concluded his report: 'The drag coefficient of the car is a very low one. Its performance amply bears out our frequent contention that a closed saloon car can be made to go faster than the conventional open sports car with the same engine. The low drag is attributable to its enclosed form, to the well-shaped windscreen and tail, and in part to the suction slot inadvertently included at the base of the windscreen. It was shown by some primitive smoke apparatus, however, that the air flow around the sides of the body is still extremely turbulent, and the least possible wind drag will not be achieved until attention is paid to this aspect of low drag design.' The slot at the base of the windscreen had been Richard Jensen's idea, and could more accurately be described as a windscreen-width vent at the rear of the bonnet panel. Richard's idea was to allow the windscreen wiper spindles to be located below the bonnet line (a styling feature found on many later cars including the Jensen-Healey), and also to let hot air escape from the engine bay and flow over the windscreen. Due to the aerodynamics of the car, however, at all but very slow speeds air *entered* this vent! But it did not matter, it still contributed to air-flow around the engine, which was the original idea anyway.

With everyone happy with the car's shape and performance, the tooling-up for body and chassis production went ahead. The glass-fibre moulds were built and the second car to be built had a glass-fibre body. This car was painted a metallic bronze colour and was registered MEA 244. It had been fitted with splined-hub wire-spoked wheels, which became optional on production models. These were of 15 inch diameter, the standard steel disc wheels being of 16 inch diameter. Jensen never offered chrome-plated wire-spoked wheels although many customers asked for them – the plating processes tended to make the spoke heads very brittle, and this was felt not to be desirable in a car which was capable of such high speeds.

The first five cars had their interiors upholstered in cream leather, with the piping matching the exterior colour of the paintwork. Subsequent models had the piping and leather the same colour, and this colour was solely the choice of the customer. If the customer required a larger driver's seat, 3 inches wider and higher could be specified, which was another example of Jensen's catering for the customer's needs.

The alloy-bodied car, JEA 541, was involved in an incident in May 1954, which led to the overdrive control being repositioned on production cars. It was press and industry day at the newly opened high speed circuit at the MIRA proving ground, and Colin Reikie had brought the 541. The car, with Reikie driving, was lapping the circuit almost flat out in overdrive top. At this time the overdrive was operated by moving the floor-mounted gear-lever further towards the driver when it was in top (fourth) gear. This movement actuated a switch that operated the overdrive solenoid. The car went into the third corner at very high speed. With the banked track forcing him sideways, Reikie's left knee touched the gear-lever, just enough to push it over and disconnect the overdrive. Instantly the transmission demanded another 1000 rpm from the engine, which it just could not provide. The rear wheels locked up and the nose of the car headed straight down the banking in spite of Reikie's instant corrective action on the steering wheel. Instinctively Reikie pushed in the clutch pedal. With the rear wheels disconnected from the engine, the car jumped about a little and then turned back in the right direction. When the smoke from the tyres had cleared he reached out for the gear-lever expecting it to be in the overdrive position. It was in the fourth gear position, of course, and Reikie realised exactly what had happened. As soon as he returned to West Bromwich plans were made to have the overdrive control moved to a dash-board stalk switch!

The Motor published their first full road-test of the 541 in September 1955. They were impressed with the style of the car and the interior fittings. 'Good looking in a business-like way,' they commented, 'neither over-ornate nor starkly plain, the two-door saloon body has been designed to accommodate four people yet to have very moderate wind resistance. It is possible to put four good-sized men in this car tolerably comfortably, rear passengers having ample foot-room, sufficient knee-room, and head-room which just suffices with nothing to spare. The rear-seat back-rest is nicely shaped to give lateral support during fast cornering. In front, the driver and one passenger will find this an exceptionally comfortable car, with bucket seats of most excellent shape. All the body interior is very bright, with good leather on the seats, and washable plastic material on the roof, doors and fascia.' Although the car was fitted with triple carburettors, a modified high-compression cylinder-head and a dual exhaust system, *Motor* explained that the Austin engine 'retained its flexibility almost unimpaired, even pulling away from 500 rpm in one of the higher gears with no protest other than momentary pinking. The figures published on the data page show very clearly the magnificent top-gear acceleration available.' The figures were certainly impressive: the maximum recorded speed was 116.9 mph, 0 to 60 mph was achieved in 10.8 seconds, 0 to 100 mph in 32.5 seconds. The overall fuel consumption throughout the test was 20.6 mpg. An interesting performance comparison lies in the Jaguar Mk VIIM Saloon, tested by *Motor* the week before the Jensen in September 1955. Admittedly the Jaguar was 5 cwt or so heavier, but the twin-cam XK engine developed some 190 bhp. Maximum speed was 104.3 mph, 0 to 60 mph took 14.1 seconds, 0 to 90 mph in 33.4 seconds, (0 to 90 mph for the Jensen was 24.5 sec) 0 to 100 mph was not recorded for the Jaguar, presumably because it took so long to get there! The Jaguar's overall fuel consumption was 18.8 mpg. The price of the two cars also made an interesting comparison: the full retail price including taxes for the 541 was £2146. 13s 4d. The Jaguar? A paltry £1679 17s 6d. This comparison shows, if anything, that though the Jaguar was incredible value for money, the Jensen equally was a *very* high performance car in its day.

The Jensen 541 De-luxe

'The unique distinction of being the first British company to market a production saloon with disc brakes fitted to all four wheels has been achieved by Jensen Motors Ltd with the introduction of a de-luxe version of the Jensen 541, for it is equipped throughout with the latest version of the Dunlop disc brakes' proclaimed *The Motor*, in their 17 October 1956 issue. 'In addition to disc brakes, the 541 De-luxe model is also fitted with a high-compression cylinder-head, twin-exhaust system, Laycock-de Normanville overdrive, and wire wheels, and its very full equipment includes a tachometer, heater and demister unit and windscreen washers.'

During the extensive testing of the 541, it was realised that the brakes were not really up to the car's full performance. At the very high speeds of which the car was capable, after fairly heavy braking into three or four bends in quick succession, the brakes could fade to an alarming degree. Alfin drums were tried (an aluminium drum with a cast-in steel liner), but as the drum got hotter, and expanded, the pedal travel increased. These drums did slow down the onset of brake fade slightly, so were offered as an optional extra, but they were not the answer and the design team started looking at disc brakes.

Girling disc brakes had been tried on the Interceptor that Richard Jensen drove, on the front wheels only. They gave impressive results, but practical difficulties were found when it came to fitting them to the smaller, 15 inch wheels of the 541 (the Interceptor had 16 inch wheels). The decision was made, therefore, to use the Dunlop system, which was well proven after Jaguar's racing experience. New hubs and caliper-adaptors were designed for the 541 application. The first car so equipped was the test demonstrator, OEA 541, which was fitted with the new brakes on all four wheels, to give the same fade characteristics, *in extremis,* on all four wheels. Strangely, this set-up did not give as efficient braking as had the earlier Interceptor with discs on the front. The braking seemed very good in traffic, but sometimes, after driving sedately along a country road, when the brakes were applied the pedal almost hit the floor. The initial reaction was that there were leakages in the master-cylinder or calipers, but the hydraulics were found to be sound. It became a severe problem, and obviously the system could not be introduced to production cars until the cause was found.

Jensen contacted Dunlop, and they sent their development engineer Harold Hodkinson over to West Bromwich to investigate. After road testing it was discovered that the pedal travel increased after a series of bends that had been taken without using the brakes. Even with Dunlop's racing experience, this phenomenon had never come to light before, probably because racing cars never went through a series of bends without using the brakes. The reason was that deflection of the rear axle half-shafts (and to a smaller extent the front stub-axles) was allowing the discs to move side-ways, pushing the friction pads apart. After one or two bends this deflection would push the pads far enough apart to produce the lost pedal travel. One more pump on the brakes would restore a full pedal, but this was not adequate on a high quality production motor car.

Most of the movement was found to be due to excessive end-float in the Salisbury rear axle, so this was adjusted down to about .003 in on the test car and as this significantly reduced the lost pedal movement, the disc brake system was pronounced satisfactory for production, and was introduced, with a number of extras as standard equipment, on the 541 De-luxe for the 1957 model year.

The Jensen 541-R

Towards the end of 1956 Richard Jensen had been lent an MG Magnette and he found that he was quite impressed with the tight steering and handling that the little car offered. Of course the MG had rack and pinion steering, and when Colin Riekie drove the car he was also impressed, and started to consider rack and pinion steering for a new version of the 541 that they were thinking about.

Jensen had heard about a new development of the Austin 4-litre engine and they felt that introducing this new engine would also be an opportunity to revise the 541 model. The engine was code-named DS7 and had quite a number of differences to the earlier DS4. It used single separate inlet ports instead of

The cover of the Jensen 541-R brochure.

A page from the 541-R brochure showing interior and mechanical details.

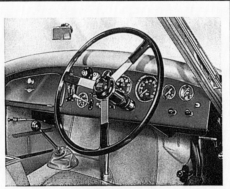

Everything is to hand for the driver of the 541 'R' Series saloon: in the restful comfort of the deeply-upholstered, finest quality hide seat the Jensen owner has all controls at his finger-tips and an uninterrupted view of the comprehensive range of instruments. Safety and ease of driving are assured.

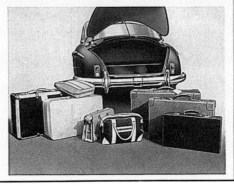

The Jensen 541 'R' Series was designed as a car eminently suitable for high speed touring and to this end was provided with a luggage boot of extraordinary dimensions for this type of car. There is ample space for luggage for four persons and such items as golf clubs can easily be accommodated. Truly this car is a combination of speed, beauty, comfort and utility without rival amongst the industry's finest products.

Safety at the high speeds of which the 'R' Series saloon is capable, can only be ensured by superb roadability and powerful fade-free utterly reliable brakes; it was realisation of the latter which led Jensen Motors to pioneer the use on *all* wheels of disc brakes by Dunlop. These brakes, introduced on aircraft, and proved in countless races, permit Jensen owners to use the full performance of their cars at all times—in complete safety.

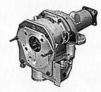

The Laycock de Normanville overdrive is an integral part of the 541 'R' Series saloon, making a valuable contribution to that silence and smoothness at speed for which the car is renowned. In addition, the reduction of engine r.p.m. for any given speed means greater economy and longer engine life, whilst the finger-tip control adds greatly to ease of driving by eliminating up to 50% of normal gear changing.

siamesed ports, and used twin SU carburettors in place of the Jensen specification DS4's triple set-up. This led to problems with the bonnet line again as the DS7 carburettors were angled upwards. The exhaust manifold as well as the carburetion was now on the right-hand side of the engine, the result of these modifications being a power output of 150 bhp at 4100 rpm.

As the decision had been made also to introduce rack and pinion steering, and sturdier suspension components, the Austin A90 front cross-member and suspension was fitted to the chassis of the 541-R prototype, necessitating redesign of the front chassis frame extensions. With the engine developing more power it was envisaged that more cooling capacity would be needed, so a completely new radiator was designed, being larger than the sloping radiator used previously. The exhaust system was redesigned as a mirror image of the original, and the battery cradle was subsequently moved from the right-hand side to the left.

Another problem with this engine was that it was only available with an automatic gearbox. Various manual gearboxes were considered but it was finally decided to use the Moss box, as fitted to the current Jaguars. The rear springs were modified to give a 1 inch increase in ride height to give more bump clearance, and the front suspension geometry and settings were similarly modified for the Jensen application.

The prototype was registered PEA 541, and was the subject of *The Autocar*'s road-test, number 1669, published on 17 January 1958.

> The latest addition to the Jensen range, the R Series 541 introduced at the London Motor Show last October, has distinguished itself by achieving in the hands of *The Autocar* the highest maximum speed of any car with more than two full-sized seats, so far provided for test. After quickly reaching 106 mph in normal top, the 541 went on in overdrive to a mean maximum of 123.5 mph and a best speed of 127.5 mph, all of this with the ambient temperature below freezing point and with a stiff diagonal breeze. The disc brakes fitted as standard all round, previously available on the de luxe 541, proved splendidly capable of bringing the car to a standstill repeatedly from very high speeds and, in conjunction with a high degree of stability, gave the green light for really fast travel on the open road.
>
> The overdrive works only on top, and the change at speeds in excess of a true 100 mph, and the immediate surge of further power as the new ratios engage are, to say the least, exhilarating.
>
> The rack and pinion steering adopted for the R Series car is to be commended. Much more precision is at hand than in the last car tested, with the results that a more delicate line may be taken and held on corners.
>
> For all its outstandingly high potential speed and surging acceleration, the R Series Jensen remains a gentleman's carriage. It has a naturally effortless gait which permits very high journey speeds to be achieved without constant use of the gears or of high rpm. While stable and safe at speed, the car is yet comfortable, and the whole conception, choice of materials and workmanship are of high quality. The model is as desirable as it is exceptional, and price is not out of keeping with character.

Rear view of the 541-R *The 541-R had slightly revised rear-end styling.*

These are a few of *The Autocar*'s comments; they were obviously impressed with the new car. The following year, the same car achieved the fastest ever time recorded by a single vehicle to travel between London and Paris. With the help of Silver City Airways, PEA 541 entered the *Daily Mail* Air Race and broke all records with a time of 2 hours 27 minutes and 17 seconds. The first stage, the 73 miles from Marble Arch to Ferryfield Airport in Kent was completed in 72 minutes. Valuable publicity for the West Bromwich factory was gained by the DS7-engine 541-R but only 53 were ever produced to this specification, as only 200 DS7 engines were produced by Austin, and most were destined for their

An interesting shot showing the subtle differences of rear-end styling between the 541 and 541-R models.

Later 541-R underbonnet view with vertical radiator and DS5 engine

Princess model. After the supply of the DS7 dried up, subsequent 541s were fitted with the DS5 engine, which again reverted to triple carburettors and a left-hand exhaust system.

The Jensen 541-S

The final, and most radical, revision of the 541 theme was introduced at the 1960 Motor Show and was known as the 541-S. Although maintaining the familiar 541 lines the body was completely restyled, being a full four inches

Special aerodynamic body designed and built by Jensen on an Austin Healey chassis for Donald Healey

The West Bromwich factory in the late 1950s.

Three examples of the 541-S model showing revised styling front and rear

wider and offering nearly $1^1/2$ inches extra head-room. Body stiffness was improved by making the windscreen surround, roof and rear panel a one-piece moulding. The most obvious change was the absence of the characteristic swivelling intake panel to be replaced by a more conventional, but less attractive, radiator grille. There was also an extra air intake incorporated in the bonnet moulding which fed the carburettors. Adjustment of air intake was still offered, now with an internal radiator blind. The 541-S was also notable for being the first British car to offer seat-belts as standard equipment, so continuing the Jensen tradition of innovation in safety.

At this point Jensen decided to change the chassis numbering sequence, by introducing a *schedule number,* which, when used as a prefix with the chassis number, would indicate the intended market and transmission fitted. The RHD 541-S had a 100/ schedule number, 102 with manual transmission, 103 for an LHD automatic model, etc.

Mechanically the 541-S continued with the DS5 engine but offered for the first time automatic transmission as standard equipment. A normal manual-change gearbox was an option but out of a total S-Series production of 127, only 16 customers preferred this. Minor changes included a rod linkage in place of the previous cable operation, a mechanical fuel pump and carburettor modifications to give smoother idling at lower engine rpm and greater economy.

The automatic transmission was the Rolls-Royce-modified version of the

The 541-R entered in the 'Daily Mail' London to Paris Air Race, July 1959

Eric Neale photographed beside his masterpiece in 1979.

General Motors Hydramatic which featured four forward speeds with full manual override on all speeds. A limited-slip differential was also fitted to automatic cars only.

Inside, the fascia was also redesigned, the instruments being concentrated in a single hooded cluster directly in front of the driver, with a glove-locker now on the left. Items included in the standard specification were a choke warning light, a fuel reserve, a variable-intensity direction-indicator warning light and an illuminated cigar-lighter. Outside, two-speed wipers, screen-washer and supplementary fog and spot lamps were now also standard equipment.

The automatic transmission and slight extra weight took their toll of performance; in *The Autocar*'s February 1961 road-test the mean top speed was down to 108.5 mph, with acceleration times suffering as well. But the report emphasised the sense of security that the driver was provided with and also the safety features built in: 'It has been suggested already that the Jensen is a very safe car. That its makers are fully conscious of their obligation in this respect is emphasized by the fact that standard equipment includes diagonal safety harness for both front seats, a small first-aid kit and a fire extinguisher.'

Safety was an aspect of car design that was always close to the hearts of the Jensen team. Standard equipment four-wheel disc brakes and seat-belts were notable Jensen firsts. Whenever a new innovation in safety was announced, it was likely to be incorporated in a Jensen motor car. However, the quest for the 'safest car in the world' was not to be realised for just a few years, and this became the ultimate development of the 541/C-V8 line, which was named the Jensen C-V8 FF.

Handsome and stylish, like the man for whom the car was built, this is the 'Clark Gable' Jensen convertible based on the Ford V8 chassis.

The S-Type Drop-Head Coupé with the hood folded.

JENSEN
One of Britain's
Finest and most
Exclusive Cars
The New JENSEN Straight-Eight 6-Seater Saloon
JENSEN MOTORS LIMITED · WEST BROMWICH · ENGLAN

Above and Above right: *Sales brochures for the 1948 PW Saloon and the PW Continental. The original artwork was produced on black card with the colours applied using chalk crayon.*

INDIA SUPER

A beautifully restored example of the first Interceptor Cabriolet.

Elegance epitomized in the PW (Pre-War) Saloon, which was powered by an Austin six-cylinder engine.

541·S

Ron Smith's well-known award-winning 541-R.

The front cover illustration and one from an inside page of the 541-S sales brochure.

The stunning but eternally controversial lines of the C-V8 are illustrated well in these pages from the MkIII sales catalogue.

ENSEN FF

is not a new car. It is a new kind of car. Under the sleekly power-packed lines of the nsen CV-8, is the formula for the future. The Jensen FF.

nce again Jensen Motors are first to lead the way towards finer cars—but this time the novation is a gigantic step into the future, even by Jensen standards. The Jensen FF th its revolutionary 4-wheel drive and aviation developed anti-skid braking system, ends speed and safety as never before. Here is a car which can be driven as no car has er been driven.

e Jensen FF opens a new era in motoring—an era of faster, safer driving. Driving the nsen FF is an electrifying experience. It gives the motorist comfort, relaxation and a w kind of confidence.

Like the P66 the original Jensen FF, based on the C-V8 chassis, advanced sufficiently for a brochure to be produced before the project was scrapped.

Sales brochure for the ill-fated P66 Interceptor. Introduced at the 1965 Motor Show alongside the FF, it shared the same fate in being shelved in favour of the Touring-styled Interceptor.

PRELIMINARY DETAILS

JENSEN *Interceptor*

This is the Jensen Interceptor. A new convertible from Jensen Motors. Designed to fill a gap in the motoring market, the Jensen Interceptor is a high speed touring car with a sporting feel. It's made for the man who likes to get around—fast and in absolute comfort. "Get up and go" tourists have never before had a car which suits their motoring outlook; but now the 2/4 seater Jensen Interceptor proves that a quiet, comfortable car can be more fun to drive than the smaller nosier type of sports car.

A very early Vignale-built Interceptor. Note the crossply tyres and the absence of the vent on the rear C-pillar.

A very stylish Interceptor MkI and its oh-so-stylish driver!

The Jensen FF MkI – the world's first really successful four-wheel-drive road car.

The 1973 SP (Six-Pack); with a 7.2-litre engine and three twin-choke Holley carburettors it produced a muscular 385 bhp.

Main pic: *The Interceptor Convertible was introduced in 1974 with no compromise occurring in the thoroughbred styling of the original.*

Above: *The rear passenger appointments of the 1987 Interceptor.*

Above right: *Walnut galore! The gleaming fascia and sumptuous cream Connolly hide of the 1987 Interceptor.*

Above: *The Hard-Top combines a new roof-line with the elegant proportions of a traditional boot.*

Main pic: *The 1987 Hard-Top Interceptor showing the latest S4 front spoiler and grille.*

Above right: *The Interceptor Coupé had a hard-top designed by Panther which utilised the rear screen from a Jaguar XJ6 and featured deep-blue tinted glass panels behind the door windows and in the roof.*

The immaculately prepared engine bay of Marco Limonci's Jensen-Healey MkI.

Main Pic: *A mouth-watering line-up of Jensens highlighting the hallmark of the marque: Style.*

The Jensen-Healey MkII, showing clearly the revised front wing arrangement.

The 1988 Interceptor interior complete with electrically powered Recaro front seats.

The Jensen-Healey MkI.

A beautiful example of the last of the Jensen-Healey line: the hatch-back GT.
The extremely practical carpeted load area of the Jensen-Healey GT.

6

The C-V8 Series

AFTER THE SECOND World War, with the business expanding, the Jensen Brothers commissioned a second factory in Stoke-on-Trent in 1947 to handle most of the commercial vehicle work. Four years later most of this work was transferred to a larger factory in Kingswinford, and after another five years the Kelvin Way factory at West Bromwich was opened. Eventually the entire operation was carried out at Kelvin Way. By the end of the 1950s the sales of commercial vehicles were slowing down, and this prompted the Tempo and Austin Gypsy contract work. The unionised labour force that was employed by Jensen was increasingly the cause of problems, as were the fluctuating sales of the 541 models. The Jensen Brothers had plans for the future though, and this was what prompted them to approach a Mr John Sheffield of the Norcros Group. Norcros was formed as a holding company, responsible for financial control of a number of firms that could benefit from the alleviation of potential death-duty problems. After negotiations Jensen Motors Ltd was put under the financial control of Norcros, which eased the minds of Richard and Alan Jensen, and also enabled them to tender for contract work secure in the knowledge that they had the financial muscle to be able to offer competitive tenders without compromising their business.

Colin Reikie had left Jensens in late 1957, having been with the firm since 1946. Eric Neale was still involved with the almost yearly updates of the 541 Series, which was the fashion dictated by market forces of the day rather than a real necessity for improvement. By 1959, Richard Jensen had many new ideas for models to replace the 541, and as thoughts had turned to that car's successor, it was decided that a new post should be formed, that of Deputy Chief Engineer. After a number of interviews, the job was offered to a Mr Kevin Beattie.

A New Appointment at Jensen Motors

Kevin Beattie was born in South Africa in 1927, but he was educated in England. He had planned to finish his education at Cambridge, where he had been accepted. Due to the death of his father, however, Kevin decided to join the Rootes Group under their Pupilage Scheme, which gave him a sound engineering base and the opportunity to gain a Bachelor of Science degree as an external pupil at London University. After many productive years with Rootes' design team Kevin was asked to join Rootes' subsidiary in Australia, to join their new and flourishing motor industry.

Kevin Beattie at his desk.

On his way to Australia Kevin contracted a serious disease which took him many weeks to recover from. Recover he did, however, and he became a key member of the Australian team. By 1958 he had been offered important opportunities with both Holdens and BMC Australia, but due to his concern for his family in England and his immediate family in Australia (his wife Eileen and their four children), Kevin decided to return home. Kevin fitted in very well with Australians and their way of life, but Eileen was not altogether happy.

On his return to Rootes in England Kevin found, as Eric Neale had on his return to Wolseleys after the War, that things were not the same. The unions were affecting Rootes' production performance as indeed they were throughout the whole British motor industry and although he gave his all to his work, as he had always done, he became desperately unhappy with the atmosphere pervading the Rootes empire.

Kevin Beattie decided that he would be far better off and could offer more, to a smaller company. He learned of the position of Deputy Chief Engineer that was being offered by Jensen Motors Ltd and, because this was the type of responsible position that he had been looking for, he applied immediately. Although a very talented engineer and a man with unbridled enthusiasm for his work, Kevin suffered from feelings of insecurity and occasionally bouts of depression. As he received no immediate reply from Jensen, this depression was heightened, but he need not have worried – he was duly summoned by Richard Jensen and after the resulting interview was offered the job.

His contract with Jensen Motors Ltd commenced on 1 January 1960 and he joined the company most enthusiastically. It did not take him long to become a key member of the Jensen team.

By the beginning of the 1960s it was becoming increasingly obvious that buyers of expensive motor cars were specifying automatic transmission. By the end of 1960 Jensen offered their 541-S with automatic transmission as standard specification, a manual gearbox being a rarely ordered option. Aston Martin were offering the option of an auto-box on their DB4 but this was never entirely successful due to the torque characteristics of their twin-cam engine. Jaguar had been offering automatic transmission for a number of years, and on their larger models fewer and fewer customers were asking for a manual gear-change.

For the Jensen application the 4-litre Austin engine was barely powerful enough to endow the 541-S with the expected Jensen high performance. Jaguar were solving the problem with the introduction of the 3.8-litre and later 4.2-litre engines, and with their massive power and torque characteristics these engines were eminently suitable for an automatic transmission. Jensen had never produced an engine of their own design so an alternative to the Austin unit was sought. The answer lay in the big-block American Chrysler V-8 engine which was supplied with the Torque-Flite automatic transmission, which was recognised as being the finest automatic transmission available.

With the Austin DS5 engine offering about 130 bhp and the 5.9-litre Chrysler engine offering 305 bhp, the opportunity was taken to design a new chassis as well as a new body. It was at this time that the beginnings of a split in Jensen's management started to develop. With the Norcros takeover, Richard and Alan Jensen were appointed as Chairmen, alternating with each other on an annual basis. Norcros had appointed Michael Day as Managing Director and this was where the beginnings of the split developed, between the Jensen brothers and employees loyal to them, and the Norcros-based management.

For the new car Kevin Beattie decided to try something he had never done before: design a chassis frame himself. He had the idea of a parallel-tube frame, using two 4 inch tubes running down the centre welded to cross-members that would support the front and rear suspension units, the scuttle and the rear seat pans. He had intended this new chassis to be lighter and cheaper to produce than earlier Jensen chassis. The idea was flawed, however, because the basic engineering advantages of the earlier peripheral-tube frame were lost, new body sill sections and outriggers having to be added to maintain overall torsional strength. Without these added sections the new chassis *was* 100 lbs lighter, but was frail and likely to twist. With the additional sills and cross-members the chassis weighed *more* than before and offered much reduced pedal-space and foot room. Nonetheless the design went into production; Eric Neale designed a new body and the title of the new car was C-V8.

The Jensen C-V8

The new model was introduced at the Earls Court Motor Show in October 1962 and immediately raised excited comment. Most of the motoring press reports praised the C-V8's impressive performance in comparison with the earlier model, the 541-S, which was still in production. The front end styling was described as 'bold' and 'could be improved' by some and 'handsome and impressive' by others. One person that was evidently not impressed with the body styling was Kevin Beattie, but he did not admit as much to either Eric Neale or Richard Jensen. The offending styling area appeared to be the headlight treatment; even so most people were satisfied, and the car still bore a strong Jensen family resemblance. As it turned out the car went into production with a headlight style that was never envisaged by Eric Neale. The decision to introduce two pairs of headlights, with the inner ones being long-range driving lights that only operated on full beam, was taken because of the new car's obvious high speed potential and new government rules that were to be introduced regarding high performance cars.

The front-end styling of the new C-V8.

Eric Neale remembers: 'My natural concern was to try and maintain good airflow and so I placed the lamps in position following the contours of the body; the smaller lamps inboard of the larger ones and mounted lower and further forward. As a designer of car bodies, to be succesful, one must create a very positive reaction from prospective customers – either love or hate, or both! I was always dismayed that in the case of the C-V8 one very important fact was never published, ie, the headlamp clusters were designed to have a pear-shaped perspex cover held in the peripheral chrome-plated mouldings, thus giving the finest airflow and appearance. However, at the last minute Richard Jensen said no, he was scared of their affecting the light emission. If I had known earlier that we were not to use the perspex covers I would have designed the headlamp layout differently, and of course there would have been no need for the peripheral chrome-plated mouldings; I would have designed separate bezels for each lamp.'

Another story that bears telling is the reason behind the idea of providing an adjustable lumbar support for the front seats. From the mid-1950s Richard Jensen had been suffering from a slipped disc. He suffered immense pain from this condition but he kept this to himself. He had such tremendous energy and enthusiasm for his cars that he would never let this condition interfere with the running of his company. Suddenly his disc would slip, usually in the afternoon, and immediately he would drive away to a farm in Shropshire where the farmer would manipulate his vertebrae to give immediate relief. Although his London doctor recommended a new operation, Richard would never consent, because he would have to have given up six months of his precious time for the operation and post-op recovery. He thus had the idea of an adjustable lumbar support consisting of an inflated rubber bag which, with the open-ended trim panel design, could be moved up or down to suit the occupant, and adjusted for air-pressure. This feature proved a godsend to many drivers, particularly Richard.

The rear seats of the C-V8 were divided by a combined arm and shoulder rest and the side arm rests had hinged tops concealing oddment compartments, the left-hand one holding the first-aid kit. The newly designed fascia was wood-faced and, as usual, very fully equipped. The large speedometer and electric rev-counter were situated in front of the driver whilst the four supplementary gauges were mounted in a central panel which was detachable to enable access to the wiring and wiper mechanism. These gauges were an ammeter, an oil-pressure gauge, engine temperature and a fuel gauge, this last named being supplemented by a low-level warning light mounted in the rev-counter dial.

The most interesting feature of the C-V8 was of course the fitment of the hugely powerful American Chrysler V-8 engine. The 'Golden Commando' was a standard specification 5.9-litre unit with the modest compression ratio of 9 to 1, quiet-running hydraulic tappets and a fairly low maximum engine revolution limit of 5100 rpm. Altogether a lazy, low-stressed engine, although very powerful and torquey, enabling a fully laden C-V8 of 34½ cwt to achieve a maximum speed of 136 mph, notably fast for the early 1960s.

In July 1963 *The Motor* commented on this aspect of the new car. 'The impression that emerged was that of a car superbly suited to Grand Touring in the true sense. A very smooth silent 6-litre Chrysler engine and automatic

The rear-end styling of the C-V8 Mk I.
The Motor *road-test car 398 KEA.*

transmission give it a performance so effortless as to be entirely deceptive. It comes as a shock when analysing the figures to find that its maximum speed of 136 mph, acceleration from rest to 100 mph in 20.9 seconds and standing quarter mile time of 15.9 seconds make it one of the fastest cars we have ever road-tested and certainly the fastest full four-seater.'

The C-V8 Series continued the new method of chassis numbering started with the 541 S. As usual, the development model was given a Jensen Motors experimental chassis number: JM/EXP 107. The first production car was 104/2001, and 104 was the intended schedule number for right-hand drive automatic models. Although other schedule numbers had been allocated for differing market areas, transmissions, etc, in practice all C-V8 models up until the introduction of the MkIII model in July 1965 carried 104 schedule numbers. The only exception to this was the three Schedule 105 cars which were produced (MkII models, right-hand drive with manual-change gear-box).

The Jensen C-V8 Mk II

Again at the October Earls Court Show (in 1963) and from chassis 104/2067, the C-V8 was revised, these revisions being very minor, concerned only with details, Selectaride adjustable rear dampers were now fitted as standard equipment, offering the driver a choice of four settings, controlled from the driver's seat. A shallow passage was built into the transmission tunnel carrying heated air towards the top of the rear seats for rear window demisting. The small sidelights had been removed from the top of the front wings and incorporated in the front indicator units which was a notable improvement. The odd looking 'door handle' situated on the nose of the bonnet moulding that

The C-V8 MkII at the Geneva Motor Show in 1964.

released and lifted the heavy panel was discontinued and replaced with a small lockable aluminium cover which concealed the lifting handle and was quite unobtrusive. At the rear of the car the only difference was the removal of the central ridge on the boot lid, giving a smooth appearance.

Mechanical specification was unchanged, but due to Chrysler's continual up-dating policy, three months later the 5.9-litre was discontinued, being substituted by a 6.3-litre (6276 cc) unit from chassis number 104/2120. This engine offered 330 bhp (SAE) which did not increase the rev-limited top speed, but made the acceleration a little more brisk.

Due to Jensen's policy of continual improvement, and the small production figures involved (there had been 66 C-V8 MkIs built), it was always a straightforward matter to introduce a change in specification when they pleased. For this reason it is quite common to look at two examples of the same model and find many minor differences, and this is the case for all models up to and including the post-1966 Interceptors. For example, during 1964 there were numerous changes to the MkII C-V8 including those mentioned above. In July the bonnet hinge assembly was altered and the previous built-in radio aerial was changed for an external unit. In September the door locking handle and assembly were changed, in November the control for the rear demister was relocated from the transmission tunnel and a chrome beading was added to the base of the petrol filler. At the same time the MkII C-V8 with manual transmission was introduced (from chassis number 2274, but with 105 schedule number).

A manual transmission C-V8 was never the subject of a published road-test (available records show that there were only three built), but on 16 April 1965 *Autocar* published their road-test of the 6.3-litre MkII, and after they had finished testing the automatic version, they conducted a brief performance test of a manual-gearbox car, for a performance comparison. 'Evidently there are still drivers so strongly against automatic transmission,' began the report, 'that they are prepared to pay more for the alternative clutch and 4-speed gearbox; this is now listed by Jensen at £100 extra including tax. After the main test was completed (of an automatic car), another car with this gearbox was put through its paces, and representative figures are included in the data. After adjustment, the clutch proved able to take the very high torque when the pedal was released abruptly at about 3000 rpm, and up to 44 mph, the limit for bottom gear, this car was slightly quicker than the automatic model. The central change, however, objects to being hurried, and although it has a positive and reasonably rapid movement for normal use, yet, try as one might, it proved impossible to make the car keep pace with the automatic one through the gears. Each change seemed to lose a full second, so that the manual model was three seconds slower to 120 mph; but it did have the edge on the automatic for maximum speed. The gear ratios are well spaced, and 97 mph can be reached in third, yet the engine is so sweet that it will even pick up speed from 10 mph (under 400 rpm), in top gear'.

Hence the reason for so few manual gearbox C-V8s (and later Interceptors with the same engine/gearbox) being built: the Torque-Flite equipped car could accelerate faster than the four-speed manual. This gearbox was, though, a standard specification Chrysler truck box, so had not been designed for quick sports car gear-changes!

MkII C-V8s ready for the paint shop. Note the glass-fibre body shells and aluminium door-skins.

In 1964 Sprite Caravans proved the stability of their product by attempting a world speed record. This is their Chief Engineer John Riseborough with his powerful C-V8 tow-car.

The C-V8 (chassis 104/2164) helped to set the new record at 101.9 mph.

The Jensen C-V8 MkIII

With the introduction of the MkIII C-V8 in July 1965, a new set of schedule numbers was also introduced. It is interesting to note that the schedule number 108 had been intended for the RHD automatic MkII with 6.3-litre engine, and was to take over from 104. Apparently, through a mistake, the wrong identification plates (from 104s) were fitted and issued before the mistake was spotted, so the revised MkIIs had to continue under the 104 schedule. The new MkIII schedule number was 112 for RHD automatic cars. Also listed was 114 for RHD manual gearbox cars but I have never ascertained if any were produced. A red MkIII with manual gearbox was seen in 1987, but not long enough to discover the schedule number.

The MkIII C-V8 entered in the Commanders Cup at Snetterton Circuit in 1965. (Kevin Beattie in overcoat with Brian Spicer behind him.)

The changes in the MkIII specification were again limited to details, but the main improvement was in the car's looks, the headlights and surrounds were redesigned, the chrome moulding was discontinued and all four headlights were of smaller, 5¾ inch, size. It provided a less fussy and much smoother front end; this is how Eric Neale would have designed the car from the start had he known that the perspex covers were not to be used.

The bumpers were redesigned and now included overriders. The side lights and indicators became separate units. The braking system still used the Dunlop four-wheel disc specification but was now dual-circuit. Inside the complete fascia was redesigned, having now been beautifully finished in burr walnut, and with more instruments and gauges in front of the driver. Eyeball face-level ventilation was also included. The front seats were fully reclining and heater outlets now fed the rear footwells. The chrome-plated external boot-lid hinges were replaced with internal ones and the name Jensen was proclaimed proudly across the rear edge of the boot-lid. On the rear panel the script C-V8 MkIII

The dashboard fascia of the C-V8 MkIII introduced walnut veneer.

Possibly the most attractive variant of the C-V8 theme was this one-off convertible. This view shows the revised front-end treatment of the MkIII series.

C-V8 convertible with the top down. Note the leather covered MkII spec. dashboard fascia, instead of veneer.

told drivers of lesser machinery that they had just been overtaken by the latest model.

John Bolster, reporting in *Autosport* in April 1966, summed up the MkIII and the C-V8 series in general: 'There are two excellent ways of going fast. For the first sort of driving you need something very like a racing car, with at least five gears, and lots of interesting noises. The other sort of fast driving demands a very big engine that you can't hear and the minimum of exertion for the driver. The Jensen is a most unusual car because, although it most certainly falls into the latter category, it is still a genuine sports car.'

The new interior was an improvement, and was designed by Jensen themselves, but earlier they had contacted Hardy Amies of Savile Row (a noted designer, though not of car interiors!) and engaged him to make the C-V8 interior more attractive without altering the shape or mechanical specification. His first attempt used seven materials of differing shades and textures, but this was found unharmonious and a little disturbing. The second attempt tried to unify the interior by using the leather colour (light-tan pigskin in the car being used to experiment upon), and dyeing carpets, headlining and all other trim to match. However, this was not deemed satisfactory either, so Jensen relied on their own good taste.

7

Contracts & Development

AFTER JENSEN Motors Ltd came under the financial control of Norcros, the management, being in a more stable position, started looking for more contract work to supplement the Austin-Healey work and the building of their own cars. The first of these was signed in 1960 between Jensen, Volvo and Pressed Steel, for body finishing, assembly and paintwork on the Volvo P1800 coupé.

This potentially great international venture, which anticipated the Japanese by twenty-five years, came about by a purely casual meeting. The Chief Sales Executive of Pressed Steel, while in Sweden, visited Volvo's factory in Gothenburg. He was surprised when the Volvo management suggested to him that his company could be involved in a venture that would have his company tooling and manufacturing a new bodyshell and thence completing the car using Volvo power train and running gear. Pressed Steel leapt at the chance, but their company was only involved in manufacturing body-shells; they needed another company to assemble, paint and finish the complete cars. There was really only one British company that had the experience, know-how and reputation that Pressed Steel were looking for; Jensen Motors Ltd of West Bromwich were contacted without delay.

Therefore in November 1958, a meeting was held at the Savoy Hotel, London, between Richard Jensen and Eric Neale, two representatives from Pressed Steel, and four Volvo agents. An initial agreement was reached, and Richard and Eric returned home to begin the design and development of Volvo's new sports car.

Twelve months later the first prototype was ready, having been built at West Bromwich by the Jensen team under the supervision and support of Volvo's resident engineer, Gösta Vallin. The Managing Director of Volvo, Mr Engallau, then visited West Bromwich and approved the prototype.

Earlier that year (1959), members of Pressed Steel's management had picked up Eric Neale at Birmingham Airport in their company aeroplane and flew to Renfrew Airport in Scotland. From there they went to the near-by Linwood factory, recently acquired by Pressed Steel, then being made ready for quantity production of the P1800 body-shell. A few months later Eric travelled to Gothenburg for a very thorough briefing covering all aspects of the contract. The final contract was duly signed, and the first body-shells were delivered from Linwood to West Bromwich. Jensen's part in the deal was to take these bare-metal shells, finish them ready for painting, and then paint and trim them to such a degree that when they were shipped to Volvo all they had to do was

The original Volvo P1800 prototype at West Bromwich.

The rear view of the same car.

add the mechanical components. Between one hundred and one hundred and fifty bodyshells went through the Jensen factory every week.

The whole idea was not without its shortcomings though. The Volvo P1800 was effectively being built in three different factories and in three different countries. There were constant disagreements on quality standards between the three contractees. The bare metal bodies that Jensen received from Linwood were needing an increasing amount of extra finishing (badly finished seams, welds, panel alignment, dents, etc), before Jensen could start their own work of painting and trimming. When Volvo received the bodies from West Bromwich there was a certain amount of damage in transit, and by the time the cars were fully built up, they were almost needing to be repaired again. It got to the stage that Volvo had to send their own inspectors over to West Bromwich to be resident at the Kelvin Way works.

Volvo soon realised that the problems were not the fault of Jensen, and they realised, especially as they were actually very short of work in Sweden, that the only way forward was to transfer the work that Jensen had been doing to their new factory in Sweden. This solved the problem as Volvo would finish the shells received from Pressed Steel themselves, and they could be assembled more fully before the painting and trimming stage was reached. Jensen were quite happy to agree with this outcome; there had been a break-clause in the original agreement, and Volvo, to take advantage of this clause, had to pay Jensen a considerable sum in compensation. Jensen continued to supply certain components to Volvo, and now had none of the problems that the contract had caused right from the beginning

Jensen's next important contract was to have its beginnings in 1959, when Rootes introduced the new Sunbeam Alpine. The designers of the Alpine had aimed at providing good performance and economy combined with comfort and they did this with some success. The resulting car was clearly a compromise (what production car is not?), but this was a successful compromise, and the result was a sporting dual-purpose vehicle. In March 1961, the Harrington Alpine, a special version of the car with hard-top body and engine modifications, was introduced to counter accusations of poor performance. This accusation would always dog the Alpine, right up to termination of production in January 1968. Rootes had always realised this, and as early as 1961, ways were being considered to increase performance. The Humber Hawk engine had been discussed, but two other engines were actually fitted to test cars: the Alfa-Romeo 1600 cc and the Diamler 2.5-litre V-8. Due to the amount of modifications that were needed to accommodate these engines, the idea was dropped by Rootes' management.

The original idea that finally provided the solution to the problem was suggested by Australian racing driver, Jack Brabham, in discussions with Ian Garrad, Rootes' West Coast manager in the United States. At the time the Ford V-8 powered Shelby Cobras were proving their might at race meeting all over America, and Brabham had many a discussion with Garrad on solving the problem of the Alpine's poor performance. Brabham felt that a V-8 engine, and the small-block Ford V-8 in particular, could provide the answer.

After discussions between Garrad, John Panks (director of Rootes Motors Inc.), Carrol Shelby and later Brian Rootes (Sales Director of the UK-based Rootes Group and son of the founder), the decision was made to commission

Shelby to build a prototype. Shelby stated that the car could be completed in two months but this was not quick enough for Ian Garrad. Therefore the first prototype was built by Ken Miles (Shelby's Chief Development Engineer, who also owned his own workshop) who managed to fit a Ford 260 ci (4.3-litre) in about three weeks. After another three weeks the prototype was starting to show true potential. Shelby had gone ahead with his prototype, which also after a lot of development was as good as Garrad had hoped for.

In the event the Shelby car was shipped to England and testing began. The Rootes team became very enthusiastic after driving the car and Lord Rootes himself contacted Henry Ford II to arrange purchase of the Ford V-8 engines. Negotiations between Rootes and Ford were finalised in November 1963, and a contract was signed calling for the delivery of 300 units per month.

At the time Rootes had neither the experience nor space to take on such a project so the decision was taken to sub-contract the work to Jensen, with their experience in developing prototypes and their production capacity. Of course Kevin Beattie had worked previously for Rootes and he knew their team and their methods very well. The development work that Jensen had to undertake was vast, involving the Rootes team, and Jensen's Eric Neale, Kevin Beattie and Mike Jones, but by the beginning of March 1964, Jensen were at the stage of fitting the engines into the developed pre-production cars.

The Sunbeam Tiger (as the car was to become known) became very successful for the Rootes Group and for Jensen. In the $5^1/2$ years of production 7067 examples were built, all but about 800 of them being exported. The financial fortunes of the Rootes Group in the mid-sixties led to the American company Chrysler taking control of 77.3 per cent of voting shares in the British company in January 1967. This was effectively the end of the Tiger project, as Chrysler quite obviously would not consider the continued production of a car that was powered by an American Ford engine.

As far as Jensen were concerned, they had realised from 1965 that the Tiger contract would likely be short-lived, due to Chrysler's ever-increasing involvement with Rootes. It was about the same time that Richard Jensen discovered that George Harriman of BMC was at loggerheads with Donald Healey, apparently considering that Healey was making too much money out of the Austin-Healey manufacture, compared to Longbridge. It was Harriman's intention to wind up the contract and fill the gap with a more powerful MG model (this was to become the ill-fated MGC).

The Austin-Healey contract had been Jensen's main source of income for quite a few years, so Richard Jensen approached his employee, friend and confidant, Eric Neale, to discuss what they could replace it with; they felt that the American market would miss the Austin-Healey, as most of the production went there, and as sales of the Jensen C-V8 would not keep the company functioning, a new volume-produced sports car in the Jensen tradition was called for.

The Jensen Interceptor P66

Eric remarked to Richard that over the years friends had said to him that they liked Jensen motor cars but they were far too expensive; when would they produce a cheaper car? This idea appealed to Richard and he and Eric spent quite a few evenings working out the form such a new model should take. It was to be entirely new, with a newly designed peripheral-tube chassis, designed to accept three different Chrysler V-8 engines: the 274 ci (4.5-litre), 361 ci (5.9-litre) and 383 ci (6.3-litre), the latter being the current C-V8 specification. The body structure was to be steel with aluminium for the panelwork.

The first prototype, a soft-top, was fitted with the 6.3-litre engine and acheived over 140 mph on test, justifying the change to aluminium for the panelwork. The car received a tremendous reception at the 1965 Earls Court

The first prototype P66 Interceptor. The wheel arches and front-end were altered for the second prototype.

Show, and many orders were placed. This prompted the building of a second prototype, this time a fixed-head, with slightly revised styling. Many words have been written and spoken of the P66 over the years and most of the criticism was of the fact that the first P66 seen at the 1965 show was a soft-top, the criticism being that most of the world's manufacturers of expensive high-performance cars were turning away from soft-top convertible models. Also the envisaged price of the car was a cause of concern; the P66 was to sell for around £1200 less than the C-V8. But they all missed the point: the Jensen Interceptor P66 was *not* to be a successor to the C-V8, it was to be a successor to the Austin-Healey 3000, and therefore carry on the tradition of the open British sports car, so much loved by the Americans. Obviously it had to be sold at a competitive price. The Jensen C-V8 was in a much higher price bracket altogether.

If the car had gone into production (which, unfortunately, it did not), it had all the ingredients of a successful recipe: it was undoubtedly British, which is what the Americans were craving for; it had a *very* high performance; it had bags of style, especially in the revised (second prototype) form; and fitted with the American engine it had instant appeal in that market, with the usual high servicing and spare parts costs associated with a foreign import being effectively dismissed.

It was at this time that the Jensen management became divided. The Jensen brothers, Eric Neale, and others loyal to them felt that production of the P66 Interceptor should commence. Kevin Beattie, Brian Owen (Norcros appointed Managing Director since 1964) and Norcros boss John Boex, on the other hand, had decided that the way forward was to employ an outside stylist to produce an entirely new model to replace the C-V8.

Beattie's theory was that the market that Jensen should be catering for was one that favoured style over mechanical sophistication. He had been very impressed with the latest offerings from Italian styling houses and thus embarked on a visit to Ghia, Touring and Vignale, and asked them to submit designs for a new body based on the C-V8 chassis.

The design that most pleased Beattie and his colleagues was submitted by Touring of Milan and it was this that Kevin Beattie put to Jensen's board of directors. The Jensen brothers and their Body Design and Development Engineer, Eric Neale, were understandably appalled by this idea, and would have none of it. However Beattie had a very strong ally in Brian Owen, the Managing Director, and they took the opportunity, while Richard Jensen was in hospital recovering from a coronary attack, to implement their proposals. By the time Richard returned to the West Bromwich works it was too late, the decision had been made.

All this had been preying on Eric Neale's mind. 'Beattie did not criticise the C-V8 styling to my face, but he certainly made up for it in later conversations,' said Eric. 'He made this his prime excuse for going 'Italian', and despite the reception of the P66 he, apparently aided by Brian Owen, wore down John Boex into acceding to his going to Italy. All three knew nothing of body design and you can imagine my feelings when I first learned of Beattie's criticisms, many years later.'

Richard Jensen echoed Eric Neale's opinion: 'Kevin Beattie could hardly be called a stylist, although he was a very good draughtsman and engineer.' It should also be mentioned that Alan Jensen retired as an Executive Director in 1963 after a serious illness, but he remained on the Board. In 1966 Richard retired as Chief Executive and Chairman on medical advice, but continued to serve on the board as non-executive Chairman.

Eric Neale was feeling more uneasy about Jensen's future prospects as time went on. He was invited by Kevin Beattie to spend four days in Italy visiting potential builders of the body shells of the new Jensen model. The Chief Engineer and the Chief Body Designer therefore left England in the spring of 1966. Eric Neale recalls, 'Kevin Beattie took me to Italy over the period 26-29 April 1966, but as I was furnished with only the minimum information, I kept a low profile. We first visited Touring in Milan for no more than four hours, and saw nothing or little of their factory or drawing office, but talked mostly to their General Manager. Kevin had a private session with him and emerged with a drawing. This turned out to be the drawing that had been accepted back at West Bromwich.

'The next day we visited Vignale's, and this was obviously a different concern to Touring. Vignale had a very lively factory which we went round extensively, seeing the methods and equipment that they used to produce all-steel bodies in varying quantities of production.'

Eric and Kevin were taken to the drawing office and Eric was introduced to the very capable designer employed by Vignale. Together they sat at a drawing board and commenced a programme of alterations to Touring's original drawings. These drawings appeared to be the work of a young designer, and needed an amount of modification before they could be considered for production. The roof line and rear windows were at least four inches longer than Eric Neale's final altered drawings, and he 'rationalised' the rest of the body to suit Vignale's manufacturing requirements. Vignale was chosen to

The revised front-end styling of the second prototype. This was early April 1966. Kevin Beattie and Eric Neale were to visit Vignale in Italy to finalise the 'Italian Car' just three weeks later.

develop and productionise the theme of the new car as they had the production capacity; Touring did not, as they were in a very shaky financial position at the time.

Eric Neale felt that as he was never involved in costing and price discussions, he was in no position to put forward the case of the P66 as a much better and quicker proposition. With two P66 prototypes already built, the cost of putting this model into production would have been many thousands of pounds less than the cost of productionising the 'Italian' car. One month later, disillusioned with the course of events and very upset at the fact that as Jensen's Chief of Body Design, he effectively no longer existed, Eric handed in his resignation to Richard Jensen. After over twenty years of dedicated and devoted work to the Jensen company, Eric Neale had had enough. Richard understood perfectly, as he was himself far from happy with recent events.

A few weeks later Eric was offered the position of Chief Development Engineer with motor body suppliers Widneys, the owners of this company, the Cheston family, being Jensen owners for three generations.

Four weeks after Eric Neale left, Richard and Alan Jensen announced their retirement. They had both been dogged by ill health for a number of years, but also felt that they had lost their company, and had no say in how it was run. It was a cruel ending to the Jensens' long career. Jensen Motors Ltd later presented Richard with a retirement gift – a MkIII C-V8. But this event was marred by someone's deciding that this particular car should be painted white;

Richard Jensen's cars had always been painted a cinnamon-grey, at his instruction. He promptly returned the car and told them to paint it his colour, which was carried out, and the car stayed in the Jensen family for many years,

The second prototype was a stylish and extremely powerful coupé; it was registered for road use and is currently undergoing restoration at West Bromwich.

leading a gentle life in Malta, and then back in England after Richard's wife Elizabeth returned after his death. She loved this motor car and only gave it up when she found that it was becoming too heavy and large for her to handle.

It was the end of Jensen Motors Ltd as a family concern, and there were many regrets. But Richard had stayed long enough to see a project through to completion that was very dear to his heart – the safest car in the world.

The Development of the Jensen FF

At the Earls Court Motor Show in 1965 Jensen had two new models on their stand, alongside the existing C-V8 MkIII. One was the Austin-Healey replacement, the Interceptor P66, and the other was called simply the Jensen FF. This car was based on a C-V8 and used a C-V8 bodyshell, but the initials FF stood for a concept in motor vehicle technology that no other manufacturer had dared to explore: Ferguson Formula – four-wheel drive and anti-lock brakes in a production high performance motor car.

Harry Ferguson Research was formed in 1950 after years of research and experimentation and had as its executive directors Harry Ferguson, the Irish tractor manufacturer and renowned racing drivers and owners Tony Rolt and Freddie Dixon. The company was formed to research and produce a four-wheel drive motor car and various chassis and power-units were experimented with. A real breakthrough came when Claude Hill, the Technical Director, designed a centre differential which apportioned the torque between the front and rear wheels. Before Ferguson's death in 1960, the company had perfected the application of the Dunlop Maxaret anti-lock braking system for motor cars, refining and developing the original aircraft system.

In 1962 an agreement was reached with Jensen Motors Ltd to use Ferguson's four-wheel drive layout in a Jensen car. This first Jensen FF was to have been a modified C-V8, but due to the Sunbeam Tiger project, the FF development fell behind schedule. The public were not to see the Jensen FF until the 1965 Motor Show. Distinguished from the normal C-V8 by the air vents in both front wings and the script 'FF' replacing 'C-V8' on the rear panel, the FF was also four inches longer, to accommodate the centre differential and transfer-case.

The rear suspension was identical to the C-V8 and included the Powr-Lok limited-slip differential. At the front, however, the suspension was radically changed; coil-spring and wishbone suspension was still used, but now with dual springs set each side of the driveshafts. A new front subframe was designed to carry the suspension, driveshafts and forward differential. Ball-and-groove constant velocity joints were used at each end of these driveshafts, the inboard joint sliding within a pot joint to accommodate plunging movement. This was chosen over the traditional sliding spline because when full power was applied the torque would bind the splines thus temporarily jamming the suspension.

The Jensen FF – the original prototype based on the C-V8.

The chassis was very different to the standard C-V8 and later Interceptor versions. It comprised a central ladder built up from two box sections which tapered towards the front. This ladder was braced by a stiff platform which reached out to the sill area and two 5 inch diameter peripheral tubes. Two 4 inch tubes travelled rearwards from this platform following standard C-V8 specification, to support the rear portion of the bodyshell. The design was exceptionally stiff for a car with such a long wheelbase.

The Ferguson Formula

The Ferguson Formula was not merely a system of driving all four wheels of a motor car – there had been many designs of four-wheel drive already in production, mostly with an agricultural accent. The Ferguson Formula was a concept that would endow a high performance car with the capacity to ensure that under conditions of rapid and sudden acceleration none of the four wheels would spin, and under conditions of severe and sudden braking, none of the four wheels would lock. These parameters were satisfied, no matter how slippery the road surface, and this was where the greatest capability of the system lay.

The basis of the all-wheel control system was a master differential and two one-way clutches. This master differential was a planetary gear that permitted a speed variation between front and rear output and also divided the torque in the ratio of 37 per cent to the front road wheels and 67 per cent to the rear. The master differential was driven by the output shaft of the Torqueflite gearbox, the rear output shaft being driven by the master differential and the front output shaft being driven through a set of Morse 'Hyvo' chains. The two one-way clutches were designed to enable the front wheels to over-run the rear wheels by 16.5 per cent and the rear wheels to over-run the front wheels by 5.5 per cent. To obtain these speed differences one clutch and its control gear revolved faster than the main shaft while the other clutch and its gear turns slower. Front wheelspin under traction was prevented by the faster running clutch which also (coupled to the Maxaret unit) prohibited rear wheels locking during braking. The slower running clutch controlled the rear wheels under traction and the front ones during braking. The possibility of all wheels locking was also prevented by the Maxaret unit sensing the mean deceleration of all four wheels. Under heavy braking in the type of slippery surface that would cause a wheel or wheels to lock, the Maxaret would sense this through its coupling to the four-wheel drive control unit and master differential. The Maxaret would then send an electrical signal to a solenoid that controlled a shuttle valve within the brake-servo, shuttling the vacuum from one side of the diaphragm to the other. This had the effect of the driver's feeling a cycling effect through the brake pedal as the pedal pushed back at him two or three times per second. This did unnerve some drivers but at least it informed them that the anti-lock was working and that they were travelling on a slippery surface.

Apart from the anti-lock system, the brakes were conventional four-wheel discs with the braking effort being biased towards the front in the ration 63 per cent front, 37 per cent rear.

The C-V8 based FF prototype was incomplete when shown at the 1965 Motor Show but the interest in the car was vast and encouraged the Jensen team to continue development. At the 1966 Earls Court Show, Jensen impressed the media and public alike by announcing the new Italian-bodied car (named the Interceptor again) and the Jensen FF, this time based on the Italian body. The FF was a production reality this time and was to provide the Jensen company with much-needed publicity the world over.

8

The Jensen Interceptor & FF

WHEN KEVIN BEATTIE finally got the go-ahead to put the 'Italian-bodied' car into production, he lost no time in putting his plans into action. After his visit to Vignale with Eric Neale, a contract was signed and a C-V8, chassis number 104/2142 (A MkII model), was sent to Italy in the late spring of 1966. The work was simplified in that the new car was basically just a body change; the chassis, drive-train and running gear were all to be left as standard C-V8 specification, and of course the glass-fibre body-work could be unbolted within a couple of hours. Shortly Vignale had built the first wooden formers for the new shell and the first prototype body was being fitted to the C-V8 chassis.

At the end of June, Kevin Beattie returned to Vignales and spent four days road-testing the completed prototype around the mountain roads of Northern Italy. Back at West Bromwich frantic preparations were being made to enable the workforce to be ready to receive the first bodyshells from Italy. As production was intended to be rather higher than that of the C-V8, there were also the resulting problems with supply of components from outside manufacturers. However, fired with enthusiasm, Kevin Beattie worked hard to

One of the first Interceptors completed with the bodyshell built at West Bromwich.

The Interceptor production line in early 1968.

solve any small problems before they became large ones. He was rewarded with the first bodyshells being delivered from Italy, fully trimmed and painted, by the beginning of October. The car was ready for the London Motor Show at Earls Court that same month. Jensen and Vignale had signed their contract, and the first car was delivered a mere six months later, which was quite an incredible feat for two small companies. The FF model was ready at the same time, and Jensen Motors Ltd were rewarded with a lot of favourable press comment and publicity for both models, even though the press day at the Goodwood circuit had been rather a disaster with most of the cars overheating!

As usual, *Autocar* and *Motor* were amongst the first to publish road-tests of the new cars, the former getting in first with a test of the Interceptor on 5th January, 1967. *Motor's* first test was exactly one month later, and this was also of the Interceptor, the first FF test being conducted by *Car* magazine in April, when they also awarded their prestigious 'Car of the Year' award to that car.

The same car, registered HEA 1D, was used for the *Autocar* and the *Motor* road tests. Both magazines were highly impressed with the performance of the Interceptor, returning 0–60 mph times of 7.3 seconds and 0–100 mph times of 19 seconds, but for some reason, when testing the maximum speed, *Autocar* could not get the car to go above 133 mph, just on the engine's red line of 5100 rpm. A month later, however, *Motor* managed to get 140 mph out of the car, with a mean top speed of 138.5 mph, which seemed to be a more representative top speed for these early cars. *Autocar* also commented on the handling: 'Almost as impressive as the acceleration and pure speed of the Jensen is the ride and handling. In town the steering feels heavy and it takes quite a lot of effort to counter the strong self-centring. As soon as the speed builds up, however, the steering lightens considerably and the quick positive response enables the car to be placed very precisely.' The test car came without power-steering, and *Motor* also commented on this. In the event, only a very few cars left the factory without power-steering, which must have been a great relief to the new owners. As with the C-V8, a manual gearbox was also specified as an option (the schedule number preceding the chassis number being 116 for these cars, rather than 115 for the standard automatic RHD version), but only 24 examples were ever manufactured. With their heavy non-power-assisted steering and equally heavy clutch release mechanisms, these cars were not for the physically weak, nor for the faint-hearted! No journal ever tested a manual gearbox Interceptor, but the 0-60 mph acceleration was reckoned to be just about seven seconds. These, then, were amongst the fastest Jensens ever produced.

Specifications

The new Interceptor continued using Chrysler's 6276 cc V-8 engine, in the same state of tune as the MkIII C-V8s. As before, the automatic transmission was Chrysler's Torqueflite three-speed, which was then recognised as being the finest automatic gear-box in the world, and could deal with ease with the engine's massive horsepower (325 bhp SAE) and torque (425 lb ft). This power was fed to the road through a Powr-Lok limited-slip differential with a final drive ratio of 3.07 to 1. Jensen stayed with cross-ply tyres in the interests of ride comfort, the Dunlop RS5 being fitted, and they proved entirely adequate until speeds of over 120 mph were reached on wet roads, when they had a tendency

The new Interceptor was constructed from small pressings welded together, resulting in a very strong construction.

The symmetrical construction meant little difficulty on the production line to change from RHD to LHD.

to start aquaplaning. Also in the interests of ride comfort, the rear dampers were again the Armstrong Selectaride units, being electrically controlled from a control on the central dash-board fascia. It seems that they were pretty much a waste of time, however, *Motor* commenting: 'On ordinary roads we could not detect much difference between the 1st (soft) and 4th (hard) settings. On bad roads, the softer induced a little more float and pitch which some people may prefer to the otherwise quicker, harsher suspension movements.'

The brakes were the servo-assisted Dunlop four-wheel disc set-up carried over from the C-V8. *Motor* stated that they were normally progressive and reassuring, but disappointing for really hard driving, proving to be juddery and about to fade during their (rigorous) test, which involved 20 crash stops from speeds around 84 mph.

The wheels were the very strong chrome-plated Rostyles with a 5 inch rim on the earlier cars, and changed to 6 inch late on in 1969, when radial tyres finally became standard equipment.

The interior was fully trimmed in leather (although some of the very early Vignale-built cars had vinyl door trims and centre consoles), with reclining front seats and deep, contoured rear seats shaped for just two people. The steering wheel was rather large and spindly, with alloy spokes and a wood-rim. The centre switch panel and gear-selector panel were veneered with walnut (although the veneer was applied directly on to the steel panel and not onto a ply-wood panel, as was more usually the case). On very early cars, including HEA 1D, there was another veneer panel on the door-trims just above the elbow-rest, but these were very rare, and it is doubtful if more than two or three were so equipped.

A rare beast – a manual gearbox Interceptor MkI.

The early MkI rear light unit; these were revised for the MkII model.

The Jensen FF

Without a doubt, the real star of that 1966 London Motor Show was the Jensen FF, based on the Interceptor, but with the incredibly advanced (for 1966) specification of four wheel drive and anti-lock brakes.

The original Jensen FF (based on a modified C-V8) had been shown at Earls Court the year before, and had caused a lot of interest. Most did not expect this new FF model to be in production before the end of 1966, and when it did go into production, it was with the brand new Italian body, which impressed them even more.

Car's road-test in April 1967 went into great detail with the FF, giving a long technical description before the actual driving impressions. Testing the development prototype, JEA 4D, they found that the performance was almost identical to the Interceptor (0-60 mph in 7.5 seconds, 0-100 mph in 18.6 seconds and a top speed of 133 mph), in spite of the FF weighing 3 cwt more. They praised the power unit: 'Once it bursts into life the engine never falters – and what a splendid unit it is! Smoothness is hardly the word for a piece of mechanism which never betrays its presence at idle by the slightest tremor, or at speed by the faintest discordant sound or movement.' Anti-lock brakes had never before been heard of on a production motor car, so this aspect of the FF came in for a lot of comment, not all of it complimentary. 'It was some time before we screwed up enough courage to try the brakes in anger, viz, on a slippery road with a known hazard ahead,' said *Car,* 'When we did, we were surprised anew at the vigorous kick-back from the pedal as the Maxaret unit went to work. It comes, provided the whole of the road is slippery and you sustain your own efforts, as a rhythmic series of jerks which shove your foot almost back to its starting point before allowing it to jam the brakes on again. The sequence is slower than we had expected, and the alarming part is that it occurs quite often during fast driving on British winter roads . . .' They concluded that, however, 'The effect is always the same: to guarantee a straight, safe stop in what one feels quite sure is the smallest possible space in circumstances which one knows full well would produce an uncontrollable skid in literally any other car.'

Tony Jacklin, Open Golf Champion, takes delivery of his FF from David Dixon, sales manager of Mann Egerton. The FF's twin side-vents are clearly visible.

It was not until March 1968 that *Motor* published their road-test of the FF, and they also commented on the disconcerting cyclic action of the Maxaret braking system. 'Nevertheless,' they commented, 'the combined four wheel drive and anti-lock braking systems displayed an impressive ability to cope with a wide variety of conditions making it impossible to lose steering control. In particular, the FF system dealt magnificently with wet and dry patches when braking heavily in a corner. In a high-speed avoidance situation, therefore, the Dunlop-Maxaret arrangement could well prove a life-saver.'

A grinning MkI Interceptor showing the low bumper line.

Of course, that was the *raison d'être* behind the Jensen FF; the flagship of their range should be the safest high performance car in the world, using up-to-the-minute technology to achieve this aim. That was the theory, but it was harder to convince the customer, as the FF cost a hefty £5340 at launch – nearly £1600 more than the Interceptor. By late 1969 the FF was priced at £7705, the Interceptor £5838, and it was this massive price discrepancy that ensured that the FF had a limited sales potential.

Specifications

The FF ran a parallel course with the Interceptor and therefore the two always had identical mechanical and body specifications, throughout any production changes, remembering of course the basic differences between the two models.

The FF was never offered with a manual gearbox, purely because the whole four-wheel-drive train had been designed and developed around the Torqueflite auto-box. The front suspension was totally different from the two-wheel-drive model, of course, but the rear suspension was the same, even though the rear axle now only had to transmit 63 per cent of the power and torque of the Interceptor. Aside from the Dunlop-Maxaret anti-lock system, the FF had Girling brake calipers, the Interceptor Dunlop. The Interceptor's discs were 11.25 inches in diameter all round; the FF had 11.38 inch discs at the front, 10.75 inch discs at the rear.

Jensen tried to make the FF look different so that the customer would feel secure in the knowledge that the man in the street would recognise that he was driving the more expensive model; but not too different, to keep production costs down. The main difference was the length: the FF was three inches longer, all of it from the windscreen pillar forward. The FF's front wings had a concave moulding running along the horizontal top edge which ran forward and down to the front bumper. There were two narrow side wing vents instead of one slightly wider example in the Interceptor. The front end styling was all slightly narrower, with the four headlights closer together and horizontal slatted grille being of a different design, lacking the angled corners of the grille fitted to the Interceptor. The grille badge proclaimed 'JFF', with no reference to 'Interceptor', as the car was known as the Jensen FF, 'FF' being the model name in the name way that 'Interceptor' was the model name of the two-wheel-drive version. There was also the brushed stainless-steel roof panel distinguishing the FF, but again, this appeared only on the earliest examples. Inside, the only giveaway was the huge transmission tunnel hump which was necessary to cover the transfer case and Maxaret unit.

Once the new model launch euphoria had died down, Kevin Beattie and his team had one or two problems to solve. Craftmanship had always been a by-word at Jensen Motors, but the early production models were not up to the usual high standard. The body-shells that Vignale had been supplying, trimmed and painted, were of such poor quality that the Jensen workforce were having to spend considerable time rectifying them, inside and out. These Italian shells were treated with very little rust-proofing, and that is one clear reason why there are very few of these early examples surviving today.

Beattie decided that enough was enough, financially as well as practically, and terminated the agreement with the Italian company. The body-jigs and press tools were transferred to West Bromwich, but this only led to more problems, as the way the Interceptor and FF bodies had been assembled and finished by the Italian workforce was deemed not suitable for the British workforce, not by Jensen, but by the unions, with their extreme job demarcation policies. After some very careful negotiations between the Jensen management and the unions, body production started, but then Jensen discovered that they had very few staff that were capable of producing a high quality body shell like the Interceptor's. These were the very reasons that Richard and Alan Jensen had been against the 'Italian-bodied' car right from the start, as they had had similar experiences over the years, latterly with the poor quality of the Volvo P1800 shells when delivered from Pressed Steel at Linwood.

It took some time to resolve these problems, but eventually they *were* solved, and production started to increase, as did the quality of each and every car.

The task of actually selling the car fell to Richard Graves, who joined Jensen from Rolls-Royce in 1966, and was to become Marketing Director. Graves realised that he had to change Jensen's marketing policy, if he was to make headway with the new car. Previously the Jensen brothers had built the cars they liked, and had hoped that others would also like them. Graves and his team right at the beginning set out to make the Interceptor the car that the market wanted, and this, therefore, affected the finished product. Between them, Beattie and Graves obviously got the concept right, and the Interceptor started selling in much larger numbers than any Jensen before.

The Interceptor & FF MarkII

Although Jensen had increased production remarkably since the launch of the Interceptor/FF (after 2½ years production was averaging 17 car per week), they were still a relatively small-volume manufacturer, and this was reflected in numerous production changes which were incorporated in the cars over the

The MkII interior was a radical change.

years. Many of these changes were minor, and proper records were never kept as to when such changes were introduced. For example, the Interceptor of mid-1969 had many detail differences to the original cars of early 1967. The opening quarter-lights were now a thing of the past, and the Jensen script on the C-panels now incorporated a vent which extracted air from the interior, the original script being set in a light moulding in the bodywork. The steering wheel had changed, being slightly smaller in diameter (power-steering was now standard), more sturdy and leather-bound. Major changes had been made to the braking and front suspension. Girling calipers replaced the Dunlop ones, and these were a great improvement, giving lighter pedal pressures and much more resistance to fade. They were the same brakes as fitted to Jaguar's newly announced XJ6, and were a much more modern and efficient design. Jaguar had also been using the Dunlop system up to the introduction of their new car. The whole front suspension set-up had been changed; the original king-pin arrangement included archaic lever-arm dampers, and dated back to the Austin Sheerline of the early 1950's. The new arrangement used top and bottom ball-joints and telescopic dampers, which gave adjustments not previously provided. At last Jensen had succumbed to radial tyres, offering Dunlop SP Sports first as an option then, later, as standard equipment. To deal with the slightly reduced rolling radius of these tyres a higher ratio final drive was specified, from 3.07 to 1 to 2.88 to 1.

The engine and gearbox combination were constantly being developed and improved by Chrysler, and encompassed five different specifications in these early years (engine series: V, B, C, D & E).

These cars were to be retrospectively known as the Mark I range, for in October 1969, the Interceptor/FF MkII range was introduced 1033 Interceptor MarkIs and 196 FFs had been produced.

Another celebrity who bought a Jensen was film star Tony Curtis, seen here with his MkII Interceptor in 1971.

The MkII cars encompassed all the refinements included in the late MkI cars, but had a host of major revisions which was the reason for the MkII badge on the front grille. The most obvious external change was the new front bumper. It was raised by 2 inches and had square overriders in place of the earlier pointed type. The redesigned side lamp/indicator units were now mounted below the bumper instead of above it. The bodywork surrounding the head-lamps was now finished in black instead of body colour. At the rear, the new overriders were included, but the button on the rear panel to open the rear hatch had been dispensed with, the hatch now being released by pulling a small lever incorporated in the driver's door-shut. The same 16 inch Rostyle wheels were used, although the rims were now silver painted instead of chrome-plated.

Further improvements included an increase in fuel capacity from 16 to 20 gallons, the fitting of new cast aluminium rocker covers with Jensen motif to the same 6.3-litre engine, a modified electrical system now incorporating 12 fuses, the inclusion of hazard-warning flashers, the replacement of the ammeter by a battery condition (voltmeter) indicator and the adoption of a lattice-type collapsible steering column. To open the fuel filler cap, you now pressed a switch on the fascia, before a key was used in the flap itself. Air-conditioning was offered as an option and was specified on the great majority of cars produced.

The main improvement in the MkII models, however, was the interior, which had been radically redesigned. The seats were entirely new, and much improved, providing the lateral support so lacking previously. Detachable head-rests were provided, which included a supplementary pad, made of foam and covered with corduroy, which was attached to the head-rest with velcro, and could be adjusted to any position that the driver required. Although at first glance the rear seat seemed unchanged, it was more deeply contoured than the MkI version.

Kevin Beattie, with Richard Graves on his right on the occasion of the 5000th Jensen (a MkII Interceptor) being completed.

Smoke from the tyres, but no loss of control – the Jensen FF in its element!

A complete redesign of the dashboard fascia resulted in the elimination of the toggle switches and their replacement by rockers, which were positioned in a bank on the centre console just above the standard equipment radio. The speedometer and rev-counter were still mounted in front of the driver, but the supplementary gauges were now mounted in a line in the centre of the fascia, all angled towards the driver. An additional glove-locker was provided on the passenger's side.

The ignition key was now part of a steering-lock, fitted just under the steering wheel, which was the leather-bound item carried over from the later MkIs. The price of the new models (to be ready for customers at the beginning of 1970) was £5838 for the Interceptor and £7705 for the FF. At the factory, the new model was differentiated by new schedule numbers: 123 for the RHD examples, 125 LHD, the FF 127.

The motoring press generally praised the MkII models, but *Motor*, testing the FF II in September 1970, made the following comments: 'Since we last tested an FF we have been lucky enough to drive such cars as a Ford GT40 and various Ferraris as well as some more recently introduced vehicles like the Aston Martin DBS and the Jaguar XJ6. It is against standards raised by the general march of progress and such particular experiences of the excellent that the FF II must be judged.

'By such standards we must confess ourselves a little disappointed in the FF II when judged purely as a machine for cornering in the dry. We feel that the sum of the small changes to the suspension has if anything a small adverse effect on the cornering, cancelling out the advantage of more and stiffer rubber on the ground. One factor which may account for the FF's slightly lurchy behaviour on corners is the adoption of dampers with a fixed setting corresponding to position 3 on the Selecta-rides previously fitted.

'Thus we don't think the FF II corners any quicker in the dry than some comparable two-wheel drive cars like a Ferrari or the Aston Martin DBS or even the Jaguar XJ6 at one third of the cost. The XJ6, of course, undermines the whole concept of the high-priced low volume luxury performance car, but it is not the price of the FF II that we object to – since it is no more expensive than some of its rivals – but we wonder whether its mechanical complexity is technically justified.' Obviously, as far as *Motor* was concerned, the press love affair with the FF was cooling, even though they recorded excellent performance figures: 0-60 mph in 7.4 seconds, 0-100 mph in 19.1 seconds, and an estimated top speed of 140 mph.

A month later, *Autocar* published their Autotest of the FF II, although not the same car as the *Motor* test. The performance figures were equally impressive (0-60 in 8.1 seconds, 0-100 mph in 21.5 seconds, with a best top speed of 141 mph, 137 mean) and they stated that acceleration times could be better by letting the engine rev higher into the red zone before changing gears, so they were directly comparable to *Motor's* figures. However, *Autocar* had no qualms about the cornering and handling abilities of the FF II: 'Mention has already been made of the FF II's remarkable traction, but we make no apologies for stretching the point. A great deal more power can be used in any given circumstances than would be possible with conventional drive. Even when deliberately provoked, the FF II rarely puts a foot wrong. Indeed, we found the limiting factor on a right-handed airfield circuit to be lack of engine power, caused by fuel starvation – a good indication of the cornering forces involved. For all practical purposes, the Jensen can be relied on to go exactly where it's pointed.'

But then this variation of viewpoint was always the case with the Jensen FF, a car that provoked controversy and discussion right from the start. This provided considerable publicity for Jensen, which enhanced sales of the cheaper Interceptor.

The Jensen Interceptor SP

After just three years of production, there were ominous noises coming from Jensen's accounts department regarding the cost of manufacturing the FF. No matter how much publicity was involved, the volume of sales could not justify its continued production. Thus a new flagship was conceived, based on the Interceptor, but with an even higher performance and higher specification. This car was to become known as the Jensen SP, SP standing for 'Six-Pack', referring to the type of carburation that was going to be used on the high performance engine.

The SP model showing the louvred bonnet and the slight increase in front end height brought about by the US headlight level regulations and introduced with the MkIII models.

The MKII Interceptor was still using the Chrysler 6.3-litre engine, at this stage the 'E' series specification. Chrysler also had available their 7212 cc engine which was available in several stages of tune. A MkII Interceptor was taken from the production line and fitted with one of these larger engines. This engine was in a much higher state of tune than the standard Interceptor engine, with a compression ratio of 10.3 to 1 (requiring five star fuel) and fitted with three dual-choke Holley carburettors. The engine developed a thundering 385 bhp SAE (330 bhp DIN), compared to the standard car's 330 bhp SAE (284 bhp DIN).

The car was developed, and the specification was decided upon. The Jensen SP was introduced at the October 1971 Motor Show at Earls Court, and Jensen saw fit to include one or two SP improvements on the standard Interceptor. Therefore the Interceptor MkIII was born, and was displayed alongside the SP. The schedule numbers were revised again, the SP being 131, the Interceptor III 128 in RHD, 129 for European LHD, 133 for US LHD. At

The alloy wheels as fitted to SP and MkIII models.

the same show was shown the FF III (schedule no 130), but this was really just to use up the final remaining FFs, there only being 15 FF IIIs built. (There had been 109 FF IIs manufactured, total FF production being 320.)

The SP was instantly recognisable from its lesser brethren by its standard vinyl roof covering and a very impressive array of louvres on the bonnet. The new 6.5 inch-wide GKN alloy wheels (also on the MkIII) looked much more modern (and enabled the fitment of GR70 tyres as opposed to ER70's on the older Rostyles). Air-conditioning was standard on the SP, as was the fitment of the Lear-Jet 8-track tape player/radio. Jensen also took the opportunity to update the interior; the dashboard remained almost the same (there were two extra eyeball vents), but the seating and door trims were totally redesigned. Central locking was included for the first time, the rocker-switch control being situated on the driver's door.

The weight of six Interceptors required an especially strong trailer unit – designed by Jensen of West Bromwich of course!

Motor road-tested the SP in March 1972. The performance figures were not as exciting as may have been hoped from the horsepower figures, but were impressive nevertheless. Sixty mph was reached in 7.6 seconds, 100 mph in 18.9 seconds and a top speed of 140 mph. The writer explained that these figures should have been better but an earlier test using substandard fuel had damaged two of the pistons! Fortunately *Autocar* had tested another SP just after its release the previous October, and had come up with more representative figures: 0-60 mph in 6.9 seconds, 0-100 mph in 16.8 seconds and a top speed of 143 mph (mean). Even so, due to the nature of the carburation, the SP never really got into its stride until it was accelerating past 75 mph. 70-90 mph was achieved in 6.8 seconds in the 6.3-litre MkII Interceptor, and 6.3 seconds in the SP. 80-100 mph took 7.8 seconds in the MkII, but only 6.6 seconds for the SP. The SP would continue accelerating strongly up to its maximum speed, but the new dual-circuit ventilated disc brakes were quite capable of pulling these speeds back without any fuss.

One of *Motor*'s few complaints was levelled at the throttle response of the six-pack carburation system. 'The operation of the six-pack system isn't entirely satisfactory,' they stated. 'Most of the time you will probably be quite content to accelerate away, albeit, still quickly, on part throttle which means just one carburettor until about 110 mph. The extra four chokes come in according to throttle position and engine load – a pressure compound system rather than mechanical. You soon know when they come in as the engine, which is hardly audible on part throttle, begins to emit a purposeful roar and you receive a firm push in the back. This sounds simple enough, but there are two side-effects; one is that response to sudden demand for acceleration when cruising slowly is a bit slow as the torque converter winds up and the carburettors gulp air to compensate for the powerful accelerator pumps; it pays to select the lower gear manually. This is all relative but when you get used to the potential acceleration you expect response to match – driven intelligently the Jensen can be very quick through traffic.

'The second side effect is more obtrusive. With the extra chokes coming in with increased engine load you can get a sudden excess of power with no noticeable throttle movement. This can happen when cruising at 110 mph and you start to climb a slight hill: the extra load on the engine is enough to open the chokes and it won't slow down until 130 mph unless you lift off first, in which case the cut-off is rather sudden. It can also happen when rounding a corner on constant throttle and the extra load provoked by tyre scrub, etc, can open the chokes in mid-corner which can be enough to dislodge the tail. When you are accustomed to these shortcomings it is easy enough to drive around them but we would still prefer a completely mechanical linkage.'

Petrol consumption, never a strong point on any of the Interceptor-based models was worth a comment from *Motor:* 'Fuel economy just doesn't really apply to the Jensen – it is thirsty at 11 mpg. At worst in France (on their maximum speed runs) we recorded 10.2 mpg, at best in England it was 14 mpg.' *Motor* summed up their test of the SP: 'Exciting performance, very quiet high-speed cruising, good road-holding and handling, well planned interior, good air-conditioning but uncertain throttle response with heavy fuel consumption.'

Like the FF before it, the SP was destined to have a short production life, this time just less than two years, the reason being that the supplies of the Chrysler Six-Pack engine had run out. This engine had been discontinued by the manufacturers because each year they were finding it increasingly hard to make it meet the stringent US exhaust emission regulations. But the SP played its part in the Jensen story, virtually being a stage in the development of the ultimate Interceptor (all of the SP 'extras' were to be fitted to the later 'J' Series as standard, excluding the Six-Pack carburettors), and today an original condition SP, with its engine in full SP specification (many were subsequently changed to a standard Holley or Carter carburettor), is a sought-after collector's item, in spite of the fuel consumption!

The Interceptor and FF MkIII

With the SP being the Jensen flagship when it was introduced in October 1971, the days were numbered for the FF model, and as stated earlier, only 15 FF IIIs were built. These FFs featured all the improvements of the MkIII Interceptors, including the new interior, alloy wheels and wider tyres. But most of them seemed to keep the MkII front bumper which had the number plate set back into it; on the MkIII Interceptor and SP the number plate was completely below the new bumper, giving the visual impression of the bumper level being raised once more. Many MkII FFs were retrospectively upgraded to MkIII specification, but a real FF III, with a 130 chassis number, is probably the most highly prized version of the Interceptor/FF range to the present day car enthusiast.

These flagship models (FF and SP) attracted a lot of publicity and the attention of motoring journalists, but they were really just a marketing ploy, to focus attention on all Jensen cars, and most motoring journalists found that the standard Interceptor performed just as well as the FF or SP in all but the most extreme driving conditions. The Interceptors were selling well, and with the introduction of the MkIII more orders than ever were being taken. When the SP was discontinued, only 208 examples had been built, but the Interceptor III

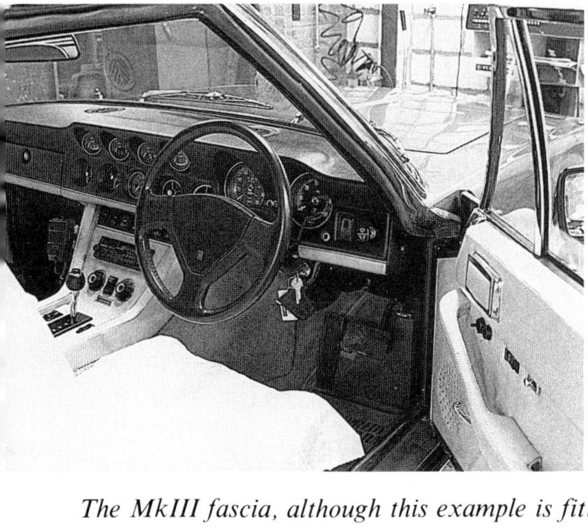

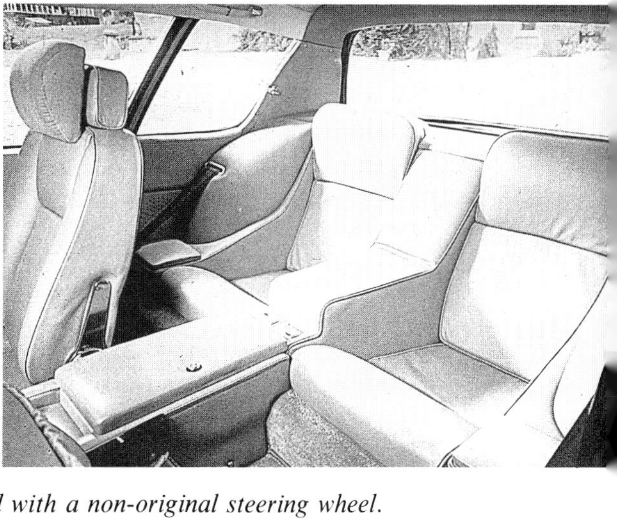

The MkIII fascia, although this example is fitted with a non-original steering wheel.

The rear seats were entirely new – and very luxurious.

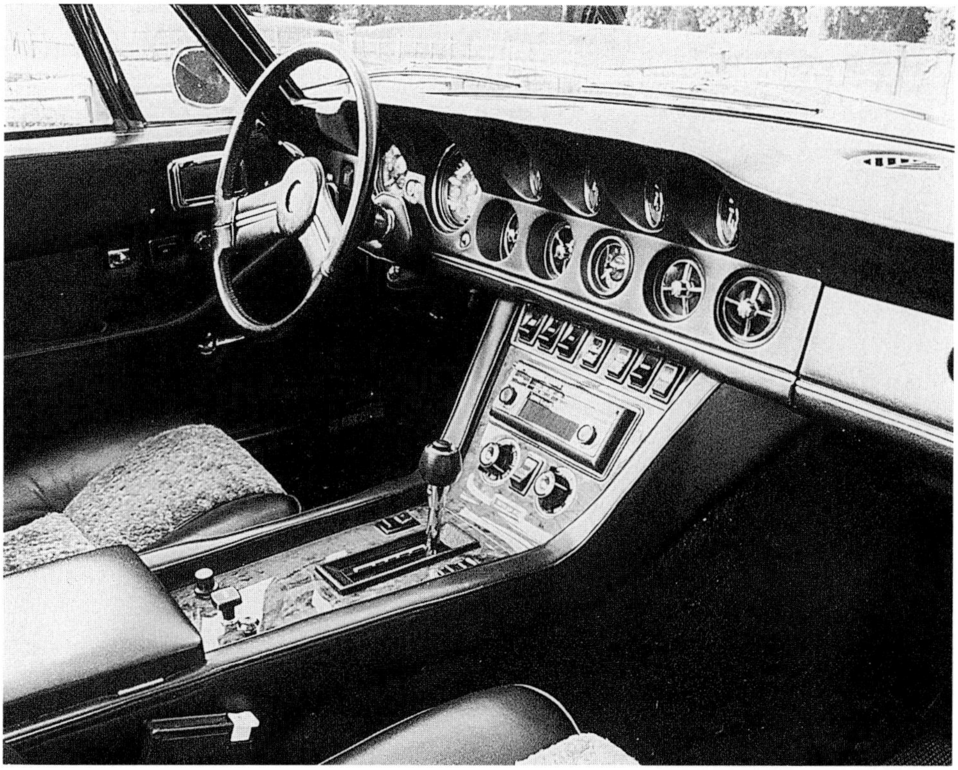

American specification interior with walnut veneer console panels and sheepskin seat inserts as standard equipment.

went on to fulfil a production figure of 3432, and that did not include the later Convertible and Coupé models.

The MkIII differed from the MkII only in detail changes, but the result was again a car which looked much more modern, and therefore had even more appeal to the customer, but under the skin there were numerous detail improvements which made for a more capable car altogether. The most important of these were the new ventilated disc brakes, 10.75 inch front and back, now operating through a dual-circuit system, which countered earlier criticisms of brake fade after repeated applications from high speed.

On the bodywork side, the front and rear bumpers were revised again, with a new single rear number plate light fitting in place of the two separate ones on the MkII. At the front, an Interceptor III badge on the grille, and new cast alloy headlamp surrounds in black, with a raised polished alloy edging around the light apertures. The characteristic wing vents also now had their fins as an alloy casting, incorporating the indicator-repeater light, which used to be placed just aft of the vent, on the wing itself. The Jensen script at the rear of the car, just below the rear hatch, was replaced with a metal and enamel badge proclaiming 'Jensen III'. The very attractive $6^1/_2$ inch wide alloy wheels completed the package, contributing to style as well as ride comfort.

Inside, although the dashboard was near-identical to the MkII, the rest of the trim had been completely redesigned. The front seats were similar, but offering more support. The rear seats were radically changed, now having a large built-in armrest between two individual buckets. The hide upholstery on all panels, including the door trims was in much larger sections than before, with no tucks or separations between sections. This design resulted in seven hides being used per interior, because of the need to use large unmarked areas of leather. Air-conditioning was still listed as an option, although most cars were being fitted with the improved system. As on the SP, central locking was now standard, and there was a three-position brightness control for the panel lights. An interesting detail was a little green light just above the ignition lock, which stayed illuminated for 15-20 seconds after the doors were closed, giving the driver enough time to find the lock and insert the key when it was dark.

The engine was the same 6.3-litre unit, now 'G' series, and later 7.2-litre 'H' series. This meant a change from the Carter carburettor used in earlier models to a Holley. These differences in engine series were not the work of Jensen, rather Chrysler's sales attitude in the 1960s and early 1970s to offer a new improved model every year. The engines were improved (or rather, their specification was changed very slightly), and of course Jensen were supplied with the engine specification that was current at the time. By 1973, due to the ever-stricter exhaust-emission regulations in the US, the 7.2-litre Holley-carburetted engine's power was down to 300 bhp (SAE), and with the discontinuation of the SP, Jensen took the opportunity to introduce the 'J' Series Interceptor MkIII, which incorporated the 7212 cc engine (in single Carter Thermoquad carburettor specification offering 330 bhp SAE at 4700 rpm), and all the equipment that had been standard on the SP would now become standard on the 'J' Series. Therefore air-conditioning (again, an even more improved set-up) was now standard on all Interceptors. The electric aerial was controlled by the radio on/off switch instead of by a separate rocker. The

The ventilated disc brakes fitted to the MkIII model.

George Segal and Richard Romanos in a scene from 'Kosygin is Coming'.

The J-Series Interceptor – note 'J' badge on rear C-panels.

Bing Crosby was in England in the summer of '75 and was lent the latest Interceptor by his golfing friend Kjell Qvale.

The Interceptor was exported to all corners of the world.

surface of the sun-visors facing the occupants was now black and the instrument panel lights had a variable-resistance control in place of the three-position switch. There were few optional extras available on the 'J' Series, but a Philips RN712 radio/cassette player was offered in place of the standard eight-track stereo radio and, for the first time, sheep-skin inserts in the front and back seats were listed; this became a very popular option. Early in 1974 a louvred bonnet (similar to that of the SP but with fewer louvres) was offered, and as the Chrysler engine fitted in the Interceptor engine bay always had a tendency to run a little hot, this was a worthwhile improvement. A J Series was distinguished from earlier MkIII's by a new 'J' badge on the C-pillars, just above the Jensen script over the vent.

One of the rare original FF MkIII's, this one owned by Dr Paul Glover.

The Jensen Interceptor Convertible

In March 1974, when almost every other manufacturer had ceased producing and designing convertible motor cars, due to their assumption that they would become outlawed by US safety laws, Jensen released what was to become a most attractive and desirable version of the Interceptor theme: the Interceptor Convertible. As it happened, the US laws never did ban the convertible, and Jensen had one of the very few luxury four-seater tourers on the market. The Convertible became popular, with over 467 examples being sold in the next two years.

The Interceptor saloon was not a shape that took readily to being converted to a soft-top, so the whole rear-end of the car was restyled with more square-cut lines and a proper boot lid. This restyling was a complete success, giving the new car a very balanced profile, especially with the hood down. The bodyshell, being mounted on the immensely strong tubular chassis, presented few problems strength-wise, when the roof was removed. Nevertheless, Jensen

The convertible version was definitely stylish, and well balanced. With the hood up the convertible lost none of its appeal, and the new rear wings and boot-lid were well suited to the rest of the car.

engineers chose to strengthen the car even further by increasing the stiffness of the body sills, also adding an additional member inside the A-posts to give more rigidity to the whole windscreen frame, and an additional strengthening plate across from one rear wheel arch to the other.

To lower the hood, the two clamps securing the hood to the top of the screen were released and the rocker-switch on the dashboard pressed. This controlled an electric motor which, with its hydraulic pump, was mounted transversely at the front of the boot compartment. The hydraulic pump operated two rams mounted just ahead of the rear wheel arches which pulled the hood irons and drew the hood back until it reached the folded position, when they cut out automatically. Continued pressure on the same switch operated the electric motors for the rear quarter windows which then lowered into the body sides. A hood cover was supplied which, when fitted, covered the folded hood. A wire built into this cover earthed through two of the pop fasteners and effectively stopped the hood mechanism operating with the cover in place. Similarly, thermal cut-out switches were included in the quarter window motor circuits and the hood motor circuit to protect them if something had blocked the quarter window cavities or the owner tried to lower the hood with the windscreen clamps still in position. The hood could not be raised or lowered unless the gear-lever was in the neutral or park position.

The rest of the mechanical and trim specification were the same as the 'J' Series, but only a few Convertibles were built to this specification, because the next stage in Interceptor developement was announced in late 1974.

With the release of the S4 Series Interceptors, not to be confused with the

The windows and frames disappeared completely into the doors.

The interior was standard MkIII . . .

Series Four Interceptors built since 1984), Jensen changed their whole chassis numbering arrangement that had followed the same pattern since the 100 schedule number of 541S in 1960. (The 'J' Series had been schedule number 136 for RHD) The new chassis numbers followed a new schedule system that used a four-digit chassis number prefix that followed a set formula. The first digit described the model type (2 = Interceptor), the second digit body style (2 = saloon, 3 = convertible), the third digit described drive (1 LHD [USA], 2-LHD

. . . although sheepskin was an often specified option.

A late walnut-dash American Interceptor convertible.

[Eur], 3 LHD and 4 RHD), and the fourth digit described market area (0 USA, Austria, Switzerland and the UK; 1 Germany and Australia; 2 France and Japan; 3 Belgium, Holland and New Zealand; 4 Hong Kong). Therefore a British specification car would carry the chassis number prefix 2240.

There were few changes between the late 'J' Series cars and the S4s. The 'J' badges on the sides had been removed, as had the 'Jensen III' badge on the back panel. In their place was a solitary 'J' badge right in the centre of the back panel, which became the exterior identifying mark of the S4. But the biggest change was inside, the previous moulded plastic dashboard panel was replaced with a magnificent new walnut example, trimmed in leather. The rest of the interior was untouched – there was little that could be done to improve it – and the walnut trim panels on the centre console were offered as options on the British cars (they had been standard equipment on US-specification cars since the 'J' Series). The steering wheel used was the one first used on later US-spec cars, which was a great improvement over the usual MkIII type.

Like the FF and SP before it, the Interceptor S4, especially in Convertible guise, became a sought after motor car, especially after production ceased, and in today's market, a low mileage walnut-dashboard convertible and a low mileage original FF III compete for the honour of being the most expensive offered for sale.

The Interceptor Coupé

Kevin Beattie, so much the driving force behind the Jensen Interceptor from the beginning, never saw the last variation on the Interceptor theme; he had been made Managing Director in July 1973, but through ill health had to relinquish this post in October the following year. He never fully regained his health and died in September 1975 at the early age of 48.

The 'Coupé' logo originated on nothing more exotic than the Morris Marina Coupé!

One of the two Interceptor 'Hard-Top' models, built by Jensen very early in 1976, just before the factory closure. This car is currently under restoration at Cropredy Bridge Garage.

The last production Interceptor was named the Coupé, announced at the London Motor Show of October 1975. It was born out of Jensen's own successful redesign of the rear panelwork for the Convertible model and the desire for a new very stylish fixed-head saloon model. Jensen turned to Panther to design the new roof line, and they modelled it to follow the lines of the Convertible with the hood raised. They used a Jaguar XJ6 rear screen and featured very dark blue tinted glass panels just behind the door windows continuing across the roof panel, the rest of the roof being vinyl covered. It was a striking-looking car in anyone's book, but the US-spec double chrome bumpers did nothing to help it. Jensen Motors Ltd was actually in receivership when the Coupé was announced; only 54 were ever built. Three prototype fixed-head models were built, which also used the XJ6 rear screen, but included the rear quarter windows of the standard Interceptor. However, by then it was too late, Jensen had ceased trading.

The Interceptor Coupé, showing the Panther designed hard-top.

9

The Jensen-Healey Years

NINETEEN SIXTY-NINE was a difficult year for Jensen Motors Ltd. With the Austin-Healey 3000 and Sunbeam Tiger body-building contracts finishing the company was faced with a crisis. The monthly turnover of around £250,000 was reduced by more than half and the company then had to make an immediate cut in its labour force, reducing it from 1200 to just over 500. The £183,000 profit of 1966 was turned into a £52,000 loss in 1967.

The problems were starting to mount up. The newly introduced Interceptor and FF were facing problems in the quality of the bodyshells being supplied from Italy by Vignale. Another aspect of the contract with Vignale was the formation in Italy of a company that would construct Interceptors from running chassis supplied by Jensen and bodies supplied by Vignale. This company, based in Turin, was headed by Carlo Dusio. These cars were to be marketed in Europe by another of Dusio's companies, Sincar. Although it had seemed a good idea at the time, the Jensen management soon came to regret it. First, the Italian-built cars were retailing much more cheaply than the UK-built cars, because of the lack of import tariffs on cars built within the EEC, and secondly the quality of the fully built cars was as bad as the quality of the bodyshells sent to the UK. The financial agreements undertaken by Vignale and Sincar with Jensen were not being adhered to, to make matters worse.

Jensen had been under the financial control of the Norcros Group since 1959 and although in its first five years Norcros was very successful, the mid-1960s had brought problems to them as well. Norcros had been thinking of selling a number of their less successful companies and reinvesting the money in more profitable concerns. At the Annual General Meeting in 1967, the Chairman of Norcros stated that a small company like Jensen was probably not a suitable investment any more. Norcros then commissioned a firm of management consultants to study all its company objectives to define the areas of profit responsibility. When the results of this study were made known, it caused Brian Owen to resign from Jensen's board, and he was replaced by Carl Duerr. His basic instruction was to decide whether Jensen should remain part of Norcros.

Duerr was born in the United States in 1916. He had had a very varied career from earning a college degree in engineering to becoming the Allied Chief of Industry in immediate post-war Austria. He later set up his business consultancy company, Inter-Counsel Establishment, in Europe. When Duerr arrived at Jensen he realised the company's serious position. Most of the management and workers realised this as well. Duerr's first task then, was to try to uplift the morale and spirit of the workers, and this he did. He seemed to them to be optimistic and always cheerful. He would talk to the staff on the shop-floor and ask for their ideas and opinions. He even took a coach-load of production workers to visit the Jensen stand at the Earls Court Motor Show later that year (1968).

The problem with the contract with Vignale and Sincar was resolved; Duerr bought out Dusio with a cash payment. He had stopped sending any more running chassis to Italy, and in future the bodyshells would be built at West Bromwich.

The next step was to organise a strong publicity campaign to counter the feelings of unease that were being felt by potential Jensen customers and also by a number of Jensen dealers. One thing he felt strongly about was the selling price of the Interceptor: he felt it should have been higher for the quality of vehicle that was being offered, and that the dealers should be aware of that fact and not be ashamed of the price that they were asking. There were also the unions to be considered. Duerr had to persuade them that 500 was still too many on the payroll, and that this would have to be reduced by 100, but production levels would have to remain the same. This was to become a further aggravation when the Interceptor body-shell manufacture was transferred to the Jensen factory. The unions, with their job demarcation policies, were not willing to commence manufacturing the bodies the way they had been made in Italy. There was the added problem of a lack of skilled metal-workers in a factory that had been producing glass-fibre-bodied cars.

Duerr eventually decided that Jensen should not remain as part of the Norcros Group. Jensen had been dealing with a public relations consultancy, Good Relations, since 1964. The Managing Director of Good Relations, Mr Anthony Good, was now also a director of Jensen. He felt that with Carl Duerr at the helm, with his highly promotable personality and skill, there was a good chance that Jensen Motors Ltd could be sold, without resorting to a foreign buyer. Tony Good was associated with a privately owned investment company, Assets in Action. This company was headed by Sir Malcolm Stoddart-Scott, then a Conservative MP, and Alfred Nathan, a City of London stockbroker. Carl Duerr, Tony Good and Assets in Action worked out a plan whereby the merchant bankers, William Brandt, Sons & Company Ltd, would acquire 100 per cent of Jensen Motors Ltd equity and subsequently pass 40 per cent of this equity to Duerr and certain directors of the Jensen board. Brandt's agreed to this, and in June 1968, Jensen Motors Ltd was under new management. William Brandt's put in their own man, Frank Welsh, as Chairman, Carl Duerr was confirmed now as Managing Director. The three other members of the board became Tony Good, Kevin Beattie and Richard Graves.

Over the next year the production of the Interceptor and FF was increased from only two or three cars per week early in 1967 to eight or nine cars per week at the end of 1969. On 14 August of that year they celebrated the delivery of the 1000th Interceptor. Jensen Motors Ltd had never before produced as many examples of one model. The London showrooms of Charles Follett Ltd, Jensen's largest and oldest established dealers, hosted the celebration. Pat Follett, Managing Director, was presented with a silver plaque to commemorate this particular milestone.

Due to the management techniques of Duerr, these 1000 Interceptors had been produced in much less than three years. However, this output of cars may have led the public to think that Jensen was a thriving business, but it was apparent to those who cared to look more closely that the opposite was the truth. Brandt's decided to mount their own investigation into the future of their investment, and they appointed another consultant, Alfred Vickers. Vickers soon learned that Jensen had a very good publicity image, due to the work of Carl Duerr and Tony Good, but the company was in a very precarious financial state: it had lost £360,000 in the previous eighteen months. Production had now been brought up to around 15 cars per week, but Vickers felt that the company could not hope to survive unless it could secure a much larger share of the available market. Vickers reported this to the board of Brandt's, and while they decided exactly what their next step was, they invited him to join the holding company as General Manager. He agreed to this, although with some reservations: he simply did not get on well with Carl Duerr.

Vickers did not make himself popular with the workforce due to his first move of declaring even more redundancies. He felt that the cars could be built to an even higher quality, in spite of Carl Duerr's work in convincing the workforce that quality of manufacture was the secret to continued success. Vickers dropped production back to about ten cars per week. He proved that ten very well made cars could be built in the same space of time as 15 indifferent ones. He had heard, within the motor trade, that Donald Healey was talking with American interests about the production of a new Healey sports car, and that Jensen had been mentioned with regard to the manufacture. Vickers felt that this could be an opportunity for the company, but that Jensen had better put their own house in order before they would have any chance of being asked to build a new car.

The New Healey

Donald Healey was rather dismayed when he learnt that British Leyland had discontinued their manufacture of the Austin-Healey 3000. It meant the end of his royalties, which his own company had been receiving from as far back as 1952. Healey had put forward a new design study for the next generation Healey sports car, but British Leyland were not interested.

Another person dismayed at this news was Mr Kjell Qvale, a San Francisco business. Born in Norway, the son of a sea captain, Qvale had emigrated with his family to the US in 1929, when he was ten years old. His business had originally concentrated on retailing MGs, but he later diversified, adding BMC, Jaguar and Rolls-Royce to his stable. The Austin-Healey had been a major success and had helped his organisation sell more than 160,000 new cars by 1970. British Leyland had introduced the six-cylinder MGC as an attempt to replace the Healey 3000, but Qvale, in agreement with most other sports car enthusiasts, dismissed this idea as unpractical, and he also realised that the MGC would have a very poor sales potential. Qvale then arranged a meeting with Donald Healey, as he thought that Healey had some influence over British Leyland, and the production of the Austin-Healey sports car. Healey explained to Qvale that his was basically a royalty agreement, and that any subsequent arrangements that BL undertook had nothing whatsoever to do with him. This was rather a surprise to Qvale, and Qvale was further surprised to learn that the bodyshells of the Austin-Healey had been built, over the years, not by BMC or BL, but by Jensen Motors of West Bromwich. Donald Healey explained to Kjell Qvale that the loss of this body-building contract was a major financial blow for Jensen, and that the company's major shareholders, William Brandt's, were now quite interested in hearing from potential buyers.

Obviously, Kjell Qvale, Donald Healey, William Brandt's and Jensen Motors Ltd themselves had a common interest. After meetings and discussions between the parties a statement was issued outlining certain changes that were going to take place. The overall majority share-holder was to become Kjell Qvale, and he would thus assume full control of Jensen. Qvale had purchased Carl Duerr's shares plus a proportion of Brandt's. In due course he was to acquire the remaining shares held by the merchant bankers. Tony Good and Kevin Beattie remained as minor share-holders and they would be joined by Richard Graves, Donald Healey and Geoffrey Healey. Alfred Vickers was appointed Managing Director, resident at West Bromwich. Donald Healey was to become Chairman, and all the other shareholders became company directors.

The statement went on to say that the production of existing Jensen models was to be increased due to the cars' being marketed in the U.S. through Kjell Qvale's distributors and dealerships. There would also begin the design and development of a new sports car in the Healey tradition. This would be sold through Jensen's existing dealers and the expanding network of international dealerships. This was April, 1970; the new car was to be called the Jensen-Healey.

Development

Kjell Qvale's idea of the ideal 'British' sports car that would sell readily in the United States was remarkably similar to Donald Healey's own views: the car should have equal or better performance to the Austin-Healey 3000, it should have better road-holding and handling coupled with a smoother ride; it must, of course, have the ability to meet all current and foreseeable future US safety and emission standards, and it must sell at a competitive price.

To ensure this competitive price, the decision was taken to use a high percentage of components currently available from large volume manufacturers. It had been decided not to consider British Leyland as a source of supply, so Vauxhall were approached as they appeared to have a suitable range of engine and suspension units. Vauxhall agreed to co-operate, so the original design was drawn around Vauxhall's four-cylinder single overhead cam-shaft 2.3-litre engine and running gear. This design had earlier been worked out by Hugo Poole, working for Healey's at Warwick. Due to the ever-changing US safety regulations, and the decision to use the tall Vauxhall power unit, Poole's original design was now becoming heavily modified. When the first prototype was produced, it received a mixed reaction from both Kevin Beattie and Kjell Qvale. They decided that this prototype design was not really what they were looking for, so they commissioned William Towns, a noted stylist, who had at that time designed the Aston Martin DBS, and was in later years to be responsible for the futuristic Aston Martin Lagonda.

Towns produced a set of drawings which were approved by Qvale and Healey. Another prototype was built, but it received a certain amount of

An early Jensen-Healey front-end styling mock-up.

criticism. This was due to the strict design conditions that Towns had been required to follow, due to the Federal safety regulations, which demanded medium-sized headlamps and tail lamps with their position fixed within fairly narrow limits, and front and rear bumpers at specified heights. These regulations influenced the whole appearance of the car. Other requirements were: ease of servicing, major mechanical units must be able to be changed quickly and easily and the outer body panels should be bolt-on, for easy repairs.

Jensen had a styling prototype to start from, so the preproduction design team was decided. Kevin Beattie was Controller and Barrie Bilbie was brought from Healey's at Warwick to be Chief Chassis Engineer. Body and chassis development work was entrusted to Brian Spicer, and day-to-day design work was entrusted to Howard Panton.

The power of the Vauxhall engine was only just considered adequate in its original form, but with the modifications needed to meet the exhaust emission rules, it was realised that the engine was going to be underpowered. Vauxhall did not help things by putting up the purchase price of each modified engine. The Jensen-Healey team then decided to look for another power-unit, talks beginning with BMW. The talks started well, with BMW offering their 2-litre engine at a reasonable price, and also offering to give an engine warranty, which would have been serviced through BMW agents. The problem was Qvale's insistence that they must provide 200 units per week, and with certain supply problems of their own, BMW could not guarantee this.

Qvale then approached Colin Chapman, at Lotus, as he had heard that they were developing a new four-cylinder engine. Chapman explained that the engine was still in the development stage and that he did not plan to offer it in a production model for about three or four years. Qvale was much impressed

Three later views of the front-end mock-up showing differing badges and wheel styles, etc.

with the specification and power output of the Lotus engine so he persuaded Chapman to offer a realistic number of engines per week, the only problem being that they were going to be expensive, and Chapman would not offer to guarantee them. The engine was very clean in relation to emission control standards, and as it was designed to be fitted at an angle of 45 degrees, it was not unduly tall.

Several versions of the engine were built and tested before Jensen arrived at their final specification. With a compression ratio of 8.4 : 1 (which allowed the use of 91 octane lead-free fuel), the United States regulations were met quite easily. The US specification engines used twin Stromberg 175 CDE carburettors mounted on a water-heated inlet manifold. The European specification engine allowed the use of two twin-choke Dellorto carburettors, which although rated at the same 140 bhp as the US engine gave better acceleration, smoothness and fuel economy.

This style was almost finalised . . .

. . . and the Jensen-Healey prototype was completed, but front-end styling was to be revised.

It was an all-alloy engine developing its 140 bhp at 6500 rpm and 130 lb/ft of torque at 5000 rpm. It featured a die-cast aluminium block and cylinder head and twin overhead camshafts driven by a cogged rubber belt operating four valves per cylinder. These valves were set at an angle of 38 degrees to each other, allowing for an efficient wedge-shape combustion chamber. At the bottom end, the crankshaft was an SG iron casting supported by five main bearings which,

The prototype's interior and dashboard-fascia.

instead of running in simple bearing caps adding nothing to rigidity, utilised a sandwich casting between sump and block.

The weight of the engine was only 275 pounds, including ancillaries. Originally it was envisaged that the Vauxhall gearbox would be used, but this unit proved to be unsuitable with its sloppy gear change and unsporting ratios. The final choice was the Chrysler four-speed unit as modified for the Sunbeam Rapier H120, this having the advantage of closer-spaced ratios. Due to the very large investment that would have been required to purchase large presses for manufacture of the unitary construction bodyshell, it was designed from the outset to be built up from a large number of small pressings which could easily and cheaply be produced by local engineering firms. The structure consisted of a floor-pan assembly of side- and cross-members bridged by corrugated panels and braced by the bodywork. At the sides there were box-section sills with central membranes for additional stiffness, while between these and the open transmission tunnel were two additional longitudinals under the floor. These were carried into a pair of beams cantilevered forward to support the Vauxhall front subframe on which were mounted the engine, steering and front suspension. The upper subframe mounting points are part way along the cantilevers which extend forwards to support the radiator and front structure. They are joined at the front by another cross-member. There was a detachable, bolt-on cross-member passing under the gearbox and supporting it, another towards the rear of the transmission tunnel. At the rear there was another box-assembly to which the upper and lower radius arms were attached. Behind this another section cantilevers rearwards to support the spring pans, the fuel tank and the boot. The torsional rigidity of this shell was rated at 2500 lb ft per degree, which was significantly stiffer than most other open sports cars without a separate chassis.

The entire front suspension, comprising double wishbones with coil springs and telescopic dampers, came from the Vauxhall Firenza, which was basically a modified Viva set-up. At the rear, the Firenza-type live axle was located by diagonal and trailing links, and suspended through coil springs and telescopic dampers. The suspension geometry was slightly altered from the Vauxhall set-up, and gas-filled dampers and shorter coil springs were specified. The standard Vauxhall stub-axles and dual-circuit brakes (disc front and drum rear) were used.

A number of different styling mock-ups were produced, but eventually the styling and mechanical development was completed and the car made its début at the Geneva Motor Show, in March 1972.

The finalised production model was rather an amalgam of ideas, a committee car, based on William Towns's original models and drawings but with afterthoughts by both Kjell Qvale and Donald Healey. Nevertheless, the new car was received enthusiastically by the motoring press. One of the first journalists to report was John Bolster, in the March edition of *Autosport*. He gave a fairly basic look at the car's specifications, but remarked that Donald Healey's latest would create a great deal of interest. *Motor, Car,* and *Road & Track* all went into lengthy description and came to the conclusion that the attractive newcomer should be a success.

Enthusiasts had to wait until 31 August 1972 before the first full road-test was published, by *Autocar*. That magazine praised the performance, ride and handling and stated that with its UK purchase price of £1810 the Jensen-Healey was bound to do well. *Autocar's* performance figures showed that the car had nothing lacking in this department: a top speed of 120 mph, coupled with lusty acceleration figures of 0–60 mph in 7.8 seconds and 0– 100 mph in 24.7 seconds. They commented that for a sports car, the ride was definitely soft, and in a different class from all other traditional British offerings. Main road bumps, uneven edges to minor roads and even the neglected kind of railway crossing were reckoned to be soaked up extremely well by the supple suspension which had more generous wheel travel than was normal for cars in that class. *Autocar* finished its road-test with the observation that the test car felt mature and fully developed, but 'much more than that, it felt like a future classic, the kind of car that one day will become a collector's item'.

Sadly, almost exactly a year later, in September 1973,*Autocar,* in their long-term test, had changed their tune. 'With 10,000 miles of Jensen-Healey motoring behind us, we confess to some disappointment. We still admire the basic concept and we accept that no company, however large, can get a complex all-new product like a motor car 100 per cent right from the word "go". But the reliability and finish of our example during its first nine months suggest that Jensen have some way to go before they can compete on equal terms with the Datsun challenge in the United States and even represent a worthwhile alternative to the longer established – and cheaper – British models in this country.' The magazine pointed out that their car was a very early example, one

Publicity shots of the Jensen-Healey in early 1972. The wheels were changed for subsequent production models.

of the first 800, but they had placed an order for it in February 1972 and they did not take delivery until January 1973. The reasons for this lengthy waiting period were claimed to be that Jensen had received a batch of faulty engines and that they had problems with supply of components. In addition, the *Autocar* car had been rejected by the dealer at its pre-delivery check because of paintwork problems. It was sent back to West Bromwich for a respray.

When they finally received their car, the *Autocar* staff were dismayed to see 800 miles on the clock. Within the next three hundred miles the car used a quart of oil. The oil consumption quickly became even worse, whereupon the car was sent back to Jensen. They tried to cure the fault but finally decided to fit a new engine. This new engine was only marginally better, and eventually new oil control rings were fitted to the pistons, which was a radical improvement. At the end of the article *Autocar* stated that they were confident that Jensen were trying to ensure that their Jensen-Healey was now a reliable and better machine than their nine-month-old example. It was to become clear, however, that engine problems were the rule rather than the exception in a good many of these early cars.

Ian Orford, present Production Director of the Jensen Car Company Ltd, who joined Jensen Motors Ltd in 1968, puts part of the blame on Kjell Qvale's insistence to Colin Chapman that Jensen must have 200 engines a week right from the start. Because of this, Chapman was not willing to give a reasonable warranty on these engines, but Qvale still accepted the deal. If there had been a comprehensive warranty involved, then perhaps Lotus would have developed, and therefore offered, more reliable engines. In the short term it was the customers that bought these early Jensen-Healeys that did the development, and this cost Jensen a lot of money.

An annoying and dangerous fault was in the Dellorto carburettors. If the car was parked facing downhill, the carburettor needles in the float chambers sometimes did not seal very well, and would leak petrol. A factory modification in mid-1973 cured this problem, however. The major problem with the engine was undoubtedly external oil leaks and therefore high oil consumption. The crux of the problem was found to be that the main oil feed to the cam housing was taken through the cylinder-head and into the cam housing through to the camshaft. The camshaft was therefore fed with oil at main oil feed pressure. There was a gasket between the cylinder-head and the cam housing, and, if this gasket failed, there would consequently be a leak of oil to the outside from the main oil gallery. This gasket did tend to be prone to leaks, as it had a tendency to creep inwards over a period of time. There were a number of attempts to cure this creeping tendency, but the problem was finally cured by adding a locating pin in the main oil feed to the camshafts, these pins retaining the gaskets in position.

A further lubrication problem was that when the engine was started from cold there would be no oil pressure reading for a few seconds. This was caused by air in the system. The oil pump was mounted externally, and overnight oil would drain back into the sump. The next morning the pump would be pumping air until it drew oil from the sump. This was overcome by drilling a 0.050 inch hole in the pressure gallery of the main oil pump. This allowed oil still present in the system to be pumped directly back into the sump, getting rid of any air-locks, and letting the pump prime itself almost immediately.

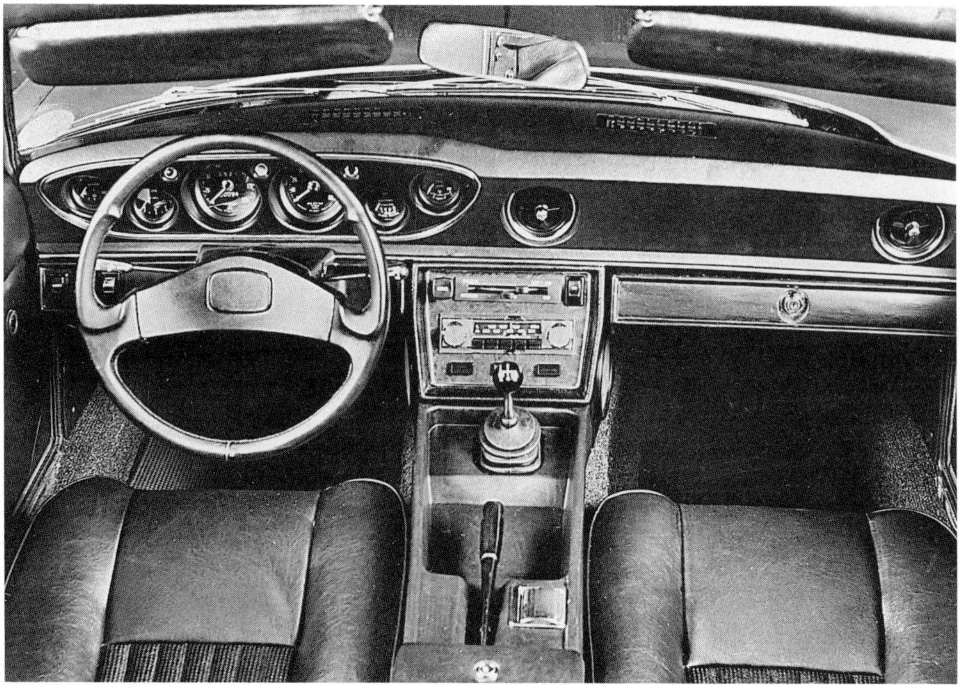

The production interior.

High oil consumption was also caused by enthusiastic owners not paying any attention to the owner's handbook. They were instructed only to check the oil when the engine was cold or at least fifteen minites after it had been stopped. Checking the oil a minute or two after the engine had stopped would give a misleading reading, as there was still a lot of oil suspended around the twin camshaft oil galleries. The subsequent over-filling of the sump would lead to oil being ingested by the breathing system, and therefore into the combustion chamber. Even though this was not really a fault in the engine design, Jensen nevertheless introduced an additional breather pipe between the inlet cam housing and the carburettor air box, which would let the sump be overfilled to a degree without the oil ingestion problem manifesting itself.

The gearbox itself proved to be trouble-free, although there were early complaints about jumping out of second and fourth gear. This was never normally a problem with the Chrysler gearbox, and it was discovered that it was due to the Jensen-fitted rubber surround over the gear lever. It was found that the surround was being compressed when the driver changed into either second or fourth gears, when the driver's hand left the lever, the rubber expanded again and threw the lever out of mesh. This was cured simply by fitting a gaiter instead of the rubber surround.

There had been many complaints from customers about the bodywork and its paint finish, but the factory worked hard in the first year of production to rectify this. Many of the complaints about rusting and poor paint finish arose from poor sealing between panels, especially between the rear wings and the rear deck. It seems that the mastik used initially would crack fairly quickly and the resulting ingress of water soon caused rusting. More effective sealer strips

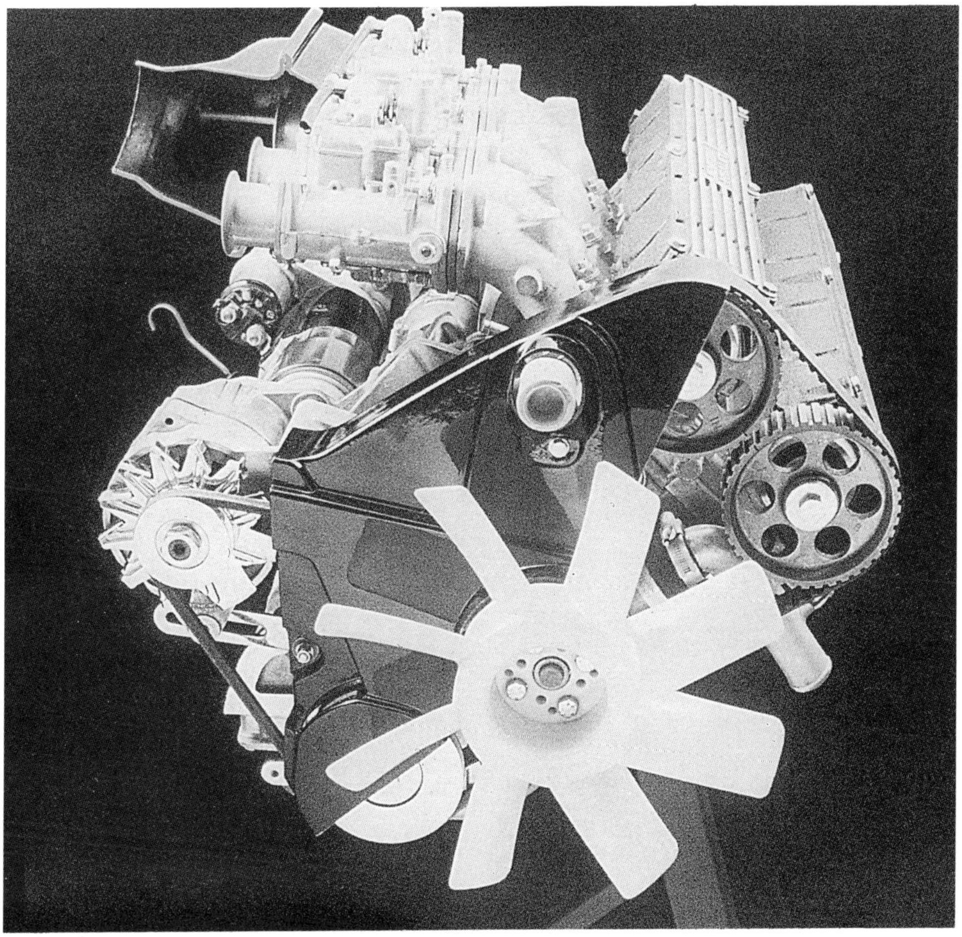

The Lotus 907 engine as fitted to the Jensen-Healey.

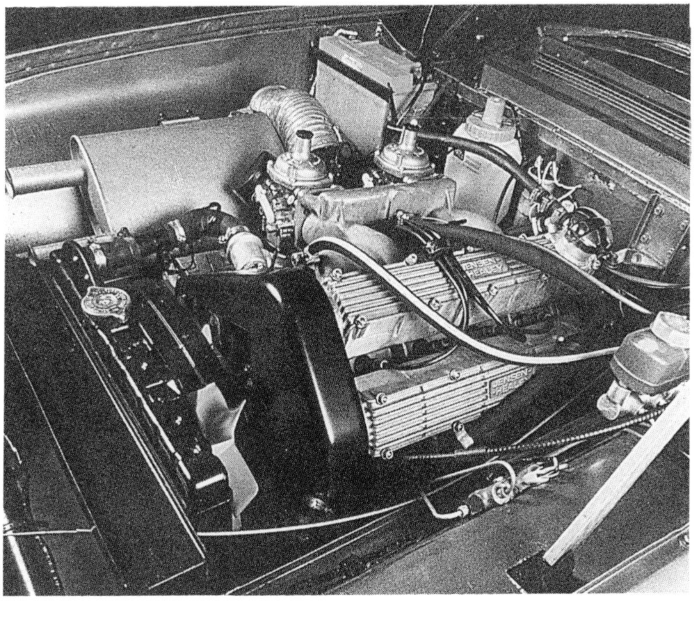

... and how it looked in situ, this car fitted with twin Stromberg CD carburettors . . .

. . . or the more usual British-spec Dellortos.

were introduced, and a sealer was introduced between the panels prior to spot-welding. Jensen also introduced a new phosphating plant and this pre-treatment eliminated most of the complaints about paint durability. Moreover, the paint process had been changed from the original air-dried finish, to a new low-bake process which gave a thicker, deeper and glossier finish.

The convertible hood, which aroused so many bitter complaints from owners of early cars was modified three times. The first modification was a slightly wider hood stick, then later the hood was again changed for a type giving greater wrap-around across the door quarter-lights, to provide greater protection against water-ingress.

Richard Graves said at the time: 'I think it is fair to say that we have taken some positive action to overcome every single defect we have noted on the Jensen-Healey. I don't think anyone can say the car has a defect we have never tried to cure. It has been a hectic eighteen months.' Jensen adopted a very generous policy on warranty claims in order to try to alleviate the sufferings of owners of the earlier cars, and to try to show that prospective owners should have nothing to worry about. This meant, however, that the factory was still paying for warranty work on cars that were eighteen months old, and therefore out of the normal guarantee period.

The Jensen-Healey Mk2

On 16 August 1973, Jensen-Healey chassis number 13352 rolled off the production line at West Bromwich. This car was yellow with a black interior, left-hand drive, American specification, and the first Jensen-Healey Mk2. As most of the production was destined for the United States, the first British-spec.

The Jensen-Healey MkII with standard bumpers.

The Jensen-Healey MkII with 5mph bumpers.

Mk2 was not finished for about another week; chassis number 13400, again yellow and black.

The Jensen engineers had the intention of putting right all the faults that had plagued the car from the outset. They pretty-much achieved this and made the car look a little prettier as a bonus. The Lotus engine was vastly improved. The Mk2 engine block was a completely new casting, offering much improved oil flow, redesigned crankshaft bearings and oil-seals. Modifications designed to improve reliability, not performance, so most road-tests reported similar performance figures for the Mk 2.

The front wings were redesigned around the head-lamp cowls, getting rid of a rust-prone joint. The joints between the rear wings and adjacent panels were given yet another sealing system, again to help stop rusting. The idea of the Jensen engineers was to provide a Jensen-Healey built to a far higher standard and quality than the early cars. As well as actually improving the quality, they wanted the car to *look* as if it was built to a higher standard. Many parts of the car were dressed up with chrome (or 'chrome-plastic') trim. This edged the bottom lip of the front and rear bumpers and the edges of the indicator light openings. A full length strip was added to the sides of the body, which became the quick way to identify a Mk2 as it hurtled past you! The inside face of the head-lamp cowl now became matt-black, and the head-lamps themselves became quartz-iodide units.

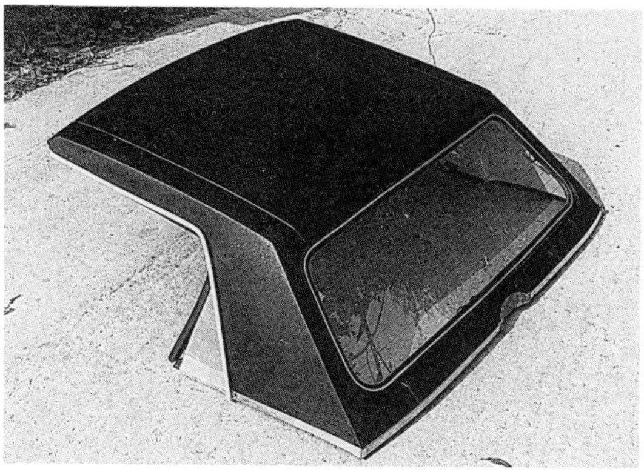

The factory hard-top offered as an option on the Jensen-Healey included a heated glass rear window.

The interior had come in for an amount of criticism, most complaints centring on the cheap plasticky look of the dash-board fascia and centre-console. This was tackled on the Mk2 by fitting a completely new fascia and console of the same shape, but a vast improvement in quality. Wood trim was fitted for the first time, albeit artificial, but with a photographic process that made the finished article look much better than some other artificial woods. This wood finish was applied to the heater control/radio panel, the switch panel and the glove-box lid. An electric clock, cigarette lighter and leather-covered gear knob were made standard equipment. The seats were made more supportive and the complete reclining mechanism was redesigned. An option of tan trim, instead of black, was offered. All these improvements had pushed the purchase price up to nearly £2500 by 1974.

John Bolster testing the Mk2 for *Autosport* commented, 'As the mechanical developments affect reliability rather than performance, I was not

A Jensen-Healey five-speed fitted with the factory hard-top.

surprised to find that the speed and acceleration of the two cars were as nearly identical as they could possibly be. The back axle of the new one was much quieter at low speeds, though the gearbox could still be heard. The engine is quieter too, though it is still pretty noisy at maximum revs – obviously the sound level would be considerably reduced with the hood down. Externally the exhaust is well silenced, thus avoiding unwelcome attention.

Real wood trim on the fascia of the four-speed MkII.

'By far the greatest improvement is in the overall quality and finish of the car, which are now commensurate with the higher price that has to be paid. If I must be critical, I would like more padding for my elbows, both on the central tunnel and the door arm-rests, while the windows call for far too much effort to raise and lower.' Mr Bolster went on to state that real progress had been made since he last tested the car.

The Jensen-Healey Five-Speed

In November 1974, Jensen introduced the Jensen-Healey five-speed model. This was effectively a Mk3, but was never known as such. There was, however, quite a number of changes, the most important being the adoption of the German Getrag five-speed gearbox.

The Getrag was a proprietary box, available in Germany as an option on some BMW models, including the 170 bhp 2002 Turbo. It was therefore more than capable of handling the Jensen-Healey's 144 bhp. This gearbox was unusual in two ways: the gear-change pattern had the top four ratios in the normal H-pattern, but first gear was out to the left and back. Also, top gear, instead of being an overdrive ratio, was a direct 1:1 ratio, as in most four-speed gearboxes. Because of this fifth-gear ratio, the Jensen engineers decided to fit a higher ratio rear axle, 3.45:1 in place of the earlier 3.727:1. The new gearbox was fitted with a propeller-shaft that used constant velocity joints in place of the

Prototype GT fascia fitted to a Jensen-Healey sports. Note the J-H seats and lack of electric window switches.

earlier Hookes-type universal joints.

In line with Vauxhall's Magnum changing to self-adjusting rear brakes, these were fitted to the Jensen-Healey at this time. In the interests of cleaner exhaust emissions the engine specification had been altered slightly. Dellorto DLH 40Es were fitted instead of DLH 40s and alterations were made to the valve timing. The most obvious external difference was the large black rubber 5 mph impact bumpers required for the US market. Inside, carpet was now standard equipment, the clock had been moved to the glove-box lid and the wood trim was now *real* wood.

Motor magazine, in their issue of 15 March 1975, complained about the pattern of the gear-change. This complaint seemed to be fashionable at the time, but this writer can find nothing wrong with this gearbox. Indeed it is one of the most positive that I have ever used, and the position of the gears is quickly mastered. *Motor* also remarked on the engine's hesitance below 2000 rpm, and this does still seem to be a problem on cars equipped with the 40E (E for emission) carburettors. They closed their article with, 'In spite of the drop in performance and economy, the Jensen-Healey is still a good, fast sports car, and outstanding when the excellent roadholding and handling are considered. The only major complaint we have is the noise, particularly that from the engine: if this could be cured – and it can, as has been shown on the Lotus Elite – it would go a long way to making the whole car quite exceptional.'

Their tested performance figures were slightly down on the previous published figures (0 – 60 mph in 8.5 seconds, but top speed still 120 mph), but this could have been due to their particular example being slightly out of tune.

The Jensen GT

The final development of the Jensen-Healey theme was the Jensen GT, introduced in July 1975, with a new chassis numbering sequence, starting at 30,001. It was not termed a Healey any more – Donaly Healey had left the Jensen Board in 1974 – and was a fixed-head, hatch-back addition to the Jensen range.

The GT was mechanically identical to the Jensen-Healey five-speed, and even used the same body panels, with the exception of the boot-lid and rear closing panel. With the extra glass, bodywork and more lavish interior trim and sound deadening materials it weighed 1.6 cwt more than the roadster, at 21.6 cwt. Not surprisingly the performance suffered slightly, *Autocar* reporting figures of 0–60 mph in 8.7 seconds, but the top speed was still the same at 119/120 mph.

In Jensen's eyes, the GT was aimed at a different sort of customer than the Jensen-Healey. This explained the new interior trim which was much more luxurious and of a far higher quality than anything seen in the roadster version. The main difference was the dash-board fascia, now a magnificent example of burr walnut veneer across the entire width. The two main dials, speedometer and rev-counter were immediately in front of the driver with the minor gauges situated two in the middle and one on each side. The switches for the heated rear window, hazard lights, rear wash-wipe, choke, lights and heater blower speeds were all situated in the large centre panel, with the heater distribution controls and 8-track tape player. Another first was electric windows with the switches on the edges of the centre console. The door-trims were thicker, and of

The stylish Jensen GT – the fixed-head hatch-back final version of the Jensen-Healey.

The walnut fascia of the GT.

a new design and the seats, front and now rear as well, were upholstered in either black or beige corduroy. These rear seats were really meant for children and did not offer very much room at all, but they could individually fold down flush to give a quite useful load area with access from the rear glass hatch. A steel sliding sun-roof and full leather trim were options.

Autocar tested the car in January 1976. They commented again on the engine's hesitance at low speeds and felt that Jensen and Lotus should have this fault sorted out by now. They were impressed, however, with the interior: 'The biggest differences between this and its forebears are seen inside. In place of that needlessly American-style dashboard, there is a handsome example of walnut veneer for the entire fascia, which raises the tone of the car tremendously. Jensen are clearly proud of the transformation; inside the pull-down glove-locker lid you find a plate declaring the coachwork to be by Jensen Motors.' They summed up: 'Generally, therefore, we liked the Jensen GT very much. That flat-spot excepted, it is a very satisfying car to drive and to run, and in the majority of opinions good to look at too. It seems quite well priced, and although there are some points which need attention, they are not by any means insurmountable by a firm of Jensen's abilities. With its equally, if differently, delightful open stablemate, it should widen the appeal of the excellent small Jensens.'

Jensen sold 473 GTs, with only 202 being registered in the UK. This brought the total number of Jensen-Healeys sold to 10,926 of which 7709 had been sold to the US market, 1914 units sold in Britain and the other 830 exported to other markets.

New model development

In late 1972, with the development of the Jensen-Healey all but completed, thoughts were turning to a replacement for the Interceptor, which had been in production for some five years. Jensen's intent was that this new car, code-named the F-type, would keep them in the front line of technology, as the decision had then been made to cease production of the FF. So the F-type was to be more expensive and up-market than the Interceptor, with a totally new aerodynamic body style, improved interior design, and completely redesigned front and rear suspension. Jensen had always been very happy with the Chrysler engine, there were very few warranty claims in connection with it, unlike the Lotus engine, so it was decided to power the F-type with the 7.2-litre version, which had full Californian emission control equipment already installed.

Jensen contacted several noted styling houses and asked them to submit design proposals. Ital Design, Bertone and Fiore submitted ideas, but it was the styling suggestions of William Towns that were again accepted. Towns' design looked very similar to the Lamborghini Espada, but had a lighter, more proportioned look, without the Espada's heavy rear flanks. Towns admitted that the Espada theme had influenced his ideas.

Towns' original 4/10 scale clay model was sent to Industor, an Italian firm of industrial designers, where they used their computer-controlled equipment to turn the dimensions of the model into full-sized working drawings. These drawings were, in turn, sent to the coach-building company, Coggilla, who fabricated a full-sized plaster model. Jensen looked at this model, decided on a

The F-type clay model on Industor's computerised drawing equipment.

few changes here and there, and then commissioned Coventry Motor Panels to build five complete prototype bodyshells.

Kevin Beattie's chief development engineer, Brian Spicer, was working on the new suspension system. The front suspension was basically a highly refined version of the standard Interceptor wishbone arrangement, but the rear was to be totally new. It was to have a de Dion axle with gas-filled struts and coil springs incorporating the Girling system of self-levelling. An Interceptor was modified to take this prototype suspension, it being made wider by four inches and longer by six inches. This car became affectionately known as 'Big Bertha'

The prototype dispensed with the central bonnet vent.

Door handle detail – MkII Escort?

Front wing styling of the F-type.

and was the same MkII Interceptor that had been used to develop the SP model.

The interior of the car was to have the most modern and highest quality trim and fittings and Jensen tried out the latest Lucas touch-controls for the dashboard fascia. William Towns later stated that when he became involved with the Aston Martin Lagonda, some of his Jensen F-type ideas were used again. The F-type was to be a full four-seater with more than adequate legroom, and the prototype had more than four inches more legroom than the Interceptor.

Jensen had tentatively registered the name *Esporanda* for the new model and had gone as far as having one of the prototypes used for roof-crush, side intrusion and barrier crash testing. One was made into a fully running prototype. This prototype was tested at the MIRA test circuit where it achieved a maximum speed of over 140 mph, this speed being governed by the rear axle ratio more than power output or aerodynamics. There was no desperate hurry at this stage to further productionise the F-type as the Interceptor was selling very well by Jensen's standards, some 30 units per week at this stage.

Some F-type bodyshells were actually built.

As the factory ground to a halt . . .

. . . bodyshells were being stored outside.

The F-type was just one of the new models being considered at this time. The Jensen-Healey's Lotus engine was now becoming more developed, and, in Mk2 form, more reliable, and thus Jensen-Healey sales were increasing. With this engine now starting to prove itself, Kjell Qvale began to look towards a car that would satisfy his idea of future market trends. He envisaged that the car to replace the Jensen-Healey would be a full four-seater, smaller than the F-type, using the Lotus engine, but designed to accept the 4-litre V-8 version of this engine that Lotus were said to be developing, when it became available. William

Towns again was asked to submit proposals, and his ideas for the G-type, as it was to become known, were for a very modern four-seater GT incorporating gull-wing doors. The same formula for the production of the first prototype bodyshell, with Industor, Coggilla and Coventry Motor Panels being involved, was used, as for the F-type. Only one full prototype bodyshell was produced.

The Mid-1970s – Jensen into Receivership

Alfred Vickers, who had joined the Jensen company in 1970, had left in July 1973. He was quoted as saying, 'The reason I left was that I never intended to stay a managing director of any company for a long period of time. I had achieved what I set out to do and that was that in the first year of my management, the company should go from deficit to profit'. In 1972, profits rose to over £200,000. But Vickers added, 'The Healey project, which had been hatched before I joined the company (referring to the original Healey design), was gradually draining it of vital finances, added to which by the time I left there were even more plans for new cars. In fact, Jensen probably had more new models on the stocks than British Leyland. There was the Interceptor replacement, a drop-head and coupé version of the Interceptor, a GT variation of the Jensen-Healey sports, plus a proposed gull-wing car. All this from a design team of four people and a production engineering department of two people.'

At this point Jensen was in an unstable financial position due to their new model development programme being paid for by loans personally guaranteed by Kjell Qvale. The sales of the Jensen-Healey in the United States were not at the level that Qvale had expected, although surprisingly, Interceptor sales were still holding up. This instability was emphasised with the "energy crisis" of 1973/74 brought on by the Yom Kippur War, in the Middle East. Ian Orford, present Production Director of the Jensen Car Company Ltd, felt that in 1975 Interceptor sales became threatened by this crisis, in the United States in particular, and up to that time the Interceptor had just about managed to produce enough profits to support the Company in the face of poor sales of the Jensen-Healey. Ian continued, 'Ironically the Jensen-Healey wasn't threatened by the fuel crisis, but nevertheless had gained something of an evil reputation in the early years which was just starting to be forgotten. Probably another year or so would have seen Jensen-Healey sales sufficient to support the drop in Interceptor sales.'

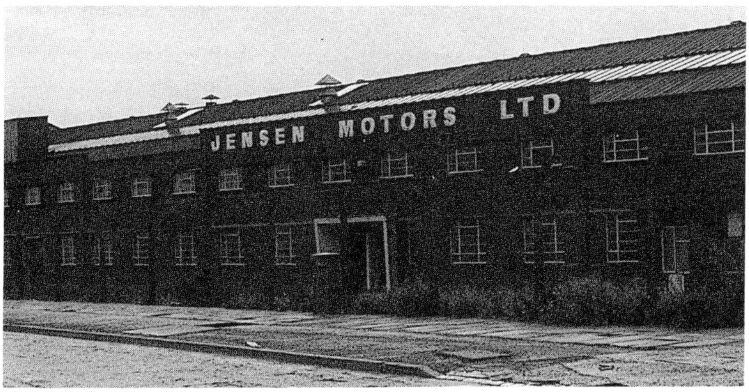

The dark days of late 1976 – a deserted Jensen Factory.

'400 workers are to be sacked at Jensen Motors' was a headline declaration by the *Daily Mail* in December 1974. The remaining workforce was put on short time. The development programme continued regardless, but the management were beginning to clutch at straws. The workforce was now reduced to around 700. Kjell Qvale was now becoming a very worried man. The new Jensen GT was rushed into production, but it did not help matters. The tooling for the car was so hastily and inadequately set up that Jensen were forced to use a high, and therefore costly, amount of labour in its construction.

In retrospect, many observers felt that Jensen might have survived the crisis in 1975 if it had not been over-extended on its ambitious plans to increase production. The company found itself in a very similar situation to that of Fodens, the commercial vehicle manufacturer. They had been forced to ask the government for assistance in the middle of their expansion drive in early 1975. If Jensen had proceeded more slowly, stepping up output of the Jensen-Healey more gradually, it might have been able to restrain its financial demands. The final factor in all this was Jensen's curious capital structure. The issued share capital throughout this five year period under Qvale, which saw turnover rise from £3 million to £14 million, remained at only £60,000. Reserves never exceeded £250,000, and the expansion programme was financed through debt, most of it falling to Qvale, with, as mentioned earlier, his personal guarantee on loans. Clearly there came a time during the inflationary spiral of 1974/75 when a halt had to be called to this kind of financing arrangement. Kjell Qvale had also started to feel that he did not have the support of the Jensen workforce. Various efforts were made to rescue the firm, but to no avail; Qvale put the company into a position where, if the directors did not want to be guilty of trading illegally, had they to call in the Receiver.

The Labour government of the time were not interested in investing money in a luxury car company. Talks started with various consortia and other car manufacturers. The Jensen GT was still being sold, the Jensen Interceptor Coupé was introduced, another version of the Interceptor, the Hard-Top, was on the cards, all whilst under receivership. Indeed many of the staff seemed not to realise (or had not been told) the gravity of the situation. In March 1976, David Millard, the Marketing and Services Director, wrote to the Jensen Owners' Club detailing the many services that the Factory could still offer the earlier Jensen owner. He outlined the attributes of the Factory Service Repair Shop, which was staffed by highly competent mechanics, bodybuilders, sheet metal workers and painters. This workshop was fully equipped and able to carry out repair work of any description on any Jensen model since the 541 series. He explained that their work was not cheap, but the final results were well worth having. He quoted, as an example, that the novelist Harold Robbins had recently had his 1968 Interceptor fully rebuilt and restored and that he was very pleased with the work.

It appeared to be business as usual. Two months later, in May 1976, Jensen Motors Ltd closed its doors. In August, an auction sale was held, and the assets were sold to the highest bidder. John Griffiths, the Official Receiver, made this statement: 'Jensen Motors Ltd, has failed for three reasons: expensive engineering was required by safety and emission laws, disappointing sales in the US market, and the high rate of inflation at home.'

It was the end of Jensen Motors Ltd – but not the end of Jensen!

10

The Wilderness Years

JENSEN MOTORS Ltd ceased trading in May 1976. Three months later a two-page advertisement appeared in the Jensen Owners' Club magazine, introducing, 'Jensen Parts & Service Ltd – the NEW COMPANY with the NEW IMAGE and the OLD JENSEN TRADITION'.

One of the tasks that an Official Receiver has to try to achieve is to make the best of what is available, with the idea of trying to pay off as many creditors as possible. To this end, two new companies were created by John Griffiths, Jensen Special Products Ltd, and Jensen Parts & Service Ltd. They were intended to be viable companies which could be, and were, sold off to help the creditors of JML.

Jensen Parts & Service's main function was to provide a parts back-up to dealers and owners; the last Jensens had been sold only a matter of weeks before, and these dealers were still having to offer a warranty, and there were obviously thousands of Jensens still on the road. JP & S also offered accident repairs (with their body-jigs and obvious expertise, they could repair certain damage that was quite beyond other repairers), servicing facilities, and also complete restoration, which was to become a very large part of their business.

The early days of J P & S were not without trial and tribulation, however. The name Jensen had lost stature, in the motor industry as well as with the general public. The very fact that the main factory had to be put into the hands of the Receiver meant a lack of confidence on the part of component suppliers who, quite naturally, were reluctant to extend credit. Added to this was the difficulty in ordering in any large quantity since there was no longer a production line to take up the excess. There was a finite number of spares that could be sold, as Jensen production had never been large by motor industry standards, and this number of cars still on the road would steadily diminish over the years. It was beginning to look as if Jensen Parts and Service would have a limited future.

Robert Edmiston, the Managing Director of J P & S, had decided that the way forward was to start distributing a new range of cars, making full use of the present Jensen servicing and parts facility. He decided that to take on a British car distributorship, in the disruptive industrial climate of the day, would not be the answer. A wide range of possibilities was examined, but Edmiston and Britcar Holdings (the holding company behind Jensen Parts & Services), decided to associate themselves with Subaru, after Edmiston's visit to Japan to talk with Fuji Heavy Industries, the Subaru manufacturing company.

Jensen of West Bromwich, but sadly no Jensens in the showroom, just Subarus and Maseratis.

Fuji Heavy Industries was the sixth largest automotive manufacturer in Japan, with sales of 150,000 units per year (Toyota at the time were selling 1.5 million units). During 1976, however, Fuji recorded a worldwide sales increase of 46 per cent! Bob Edmiston said at the time, 'We are confident that the new range will quickly establish for itself in Great Britain, the same reputation for quality and reliability that it has established in other countries. Subaru has already made substantial sales progress in Belgium and Norway where it was only introduced quite recently. This has followed the pattern which has been set in such areas as Australia and the United States where it is now a household name.'

A new company was formed, Subaru UK Ltd, a subsidiary of JP & S., and Edmiston was made Managing Director. This company started distributing towards the end of 1977. The original intention was to distribute through existing Jensen dealers, but not all of these dealers wished to co-operate, so new outlets were sought.

The holding company, Britcar Holdings, had been set up and financed mainly by Kjell Qvale, with a small interest from some of the ex-directors of Jensen Motors. Tony Good was one of these, still having some faith in the future of a small firm building luxury cars. When asked whether the Jensen Interceptor might raise its head again he stated simply, 'Britcar Holdings have bought all the tooling for the Interceptor from the Receiver . . .'

Tony Good's (and the rest of the Britcar consortium's) original idea had been to buy Jensen Motors from the Receiver, and indeed, they raised enough money to do this. They did not really have any working capital, however, and the decision was taken to purchase Jensen Special Products (a specialist light engineering and design firm consisting essentially of the old Jensen Motors engineering development department) and Jensen Parts and Service. There were a few ideas in the first year to try to develop a new Jensen-Healey sized car, but they did not come to fruitition.

There were however still Interceptors awaiting service at the workshops of Jensen Parts & Service.

The busy Jensen Parts & Service workshop.

Another shot of the workshop with a Coupé in the foreground.

In the summer of 1978, Chantry-Keys Industrial Estates Ltd paid nearly £850,000 for the Jensen Motors Factory, which had been lying idle. The factory was converted into an industrial estate, with units ranging in size from 3000 sq ft to 140,000 sq ft. Jensen Special Products remained on the site, but the writing was on the wall for that particular company.

Jensen Parts & Service was continuing to survive quite nicely, with Subarus selling reasonably successfully. This prompted them to form another company, International Motors Ltd, to import and distribute foreign cars, adding Maserati, and later Hyundai, to their stable. In 1981, International Motors decided to move out from Kelvin Way, into a new factory a couple of miles

Into the 1980s, restoration became increasingly important to JPS.

An Interceptor awaiting completion during full restoration.

away, leaving just Jensen Parts & Service remaining in the old service department building of Jensen's.

Edmiston was now totally involved with International Motors, and in June 1982 he sold Jensen Parts & Service (together with a solus user-agreement for the names, Jensen, Interceptor, Jensen-Healey and all the associated designs and logos) to Ian Orford, who thus became the Managing Director. Orford had been involved with Jensen for a number of years, originally having joined Jensen Motors Ltd in 1968, when the Interceptor was in its second year of production.

The Interceptor Reborn

Ian Orford was a man with an idea. And as soon as he had bought JP & S he started to bring this idea towards reality. The idea was simple: to build a brand new Jensen Interceptor – but the reality was somewhat different. It took longer than originally envisaged to complete the first car, but it was ready for display at London's Motorfair show in late 1983. It took many by surprise, but the press and public alike were enthusiastic. Here it was, in 1983, seven years after the original factory closed, a *new* Interceptor, not restored, and offered for sale, with the promise of more to come.

The new car was unveiled by Lord Strathcarron, a Jensen owner and enthusiast for many years. 'This is a memorable occasion for all those who admired the Jensen car,' said Lord Strathcarron, 'and who were very sad when production ceased in 1976. During the intervening years the Jensen Owners' Club, of which I am proud to be President, has done much to further the enthusiasm and interest which has always been part of Jensen ownership. Jensen Parts & Service, under the guidance of Ian Orford, have continued to service and look after Jensens during the past seven years.

By 1984 it was Jensen Cars Ltd, still at Kelvin Way, West Bromwich.

Jensen Cars' trim shop . . . *. . . illustrating that Jensen craftsmanship continues.*

'This is a most happy occasion for we are about to see once again a brand new Jensen Interceptor. Before unveiling it, I should like to pay tribute to the enterprise and hard work which has gone into this project and also to those members of the Jensen Owners' Club who have lent their immaculate cars in support.

'I have much pleasure in unveiling the first of the new Jensens – but before doing so, would like to mention that this is the same dust sheet which was used to cover the first Interceptor in 1966.'

The interest and enthusiasm shown in this new car prompted Orford and his team to embark on a programme to make the car ready for production on a limited basis, by solving the problems that they had found in procuring certain parts, and by settling on a standard specification. Six months later their plans had been pretty much finalised, and Ian Orford wrote to the Jensen Owners' Club to inform them of progress: 'Our production plans call for two vehicles, a Saloon and a Convertible, to the new "Series Four" specification (Orford had found that there needed to be so many changes in the specification of the new cars, that they were obviously not just the same car as the late Mark IIIs, hence Series Four), to be ready for the Motor Show at the National Exhibition Centre in October. Space is booked, and if all goes to plan we shall be there as a fully fledged manufacturer exhibiting fully type-approved vehicles, and under our new name of Jensen Cars Ltd.

'Charles Follet of London have been granted the sole UK distribution rights, and will take delivery of these two new cars immediately after the show. As sold in the UK, and including all UK taxes, delivery, etc, the Saloon will retail at around £40,000, the Convertible at around £45,000.

'Many of the changes we have made to the cars I naturally wish to withhold from release till after. Suffice it to say, the intrinsic character of the car will not be diminished in any way, indeed we feel the changes made will add immeasurably to the overall concept of the car, and therefore its acceptance, to the discriminating motorists who will be our customers.

'Those then are our plans for 1984. For 1985 we plan to deliver five vehicles to Follets. For 1986, ten vehicles and thereafter twelve per year.

'All our cars will be specifically made for the customer, and already we have finalised basic details of the first twelve. In many ways, it seems that history is repeating itself, as this was indeed the way the Jensen Brothers made their name originally, building very high quality, exclusive cars for the man or woman who wants the best car available, combined with elegance, comfort and an unostentatious appearance.'

In retrospect, Orford's intentions were just a little too ambitious, with just 16 cars being sold by the end of 1987. But sell they did, on a limited basis.

The Jensen Interceptor Series Four

Trying to put a motor vehicle into production again after an eight year lapse, especially a specialised coachbuilt vehicle like a Jensen Interceptor, was no easy task. There was no problem with the bodyshell itself, remembering that Jensen Parts & Service had bought all the body-jigs and tooling from the Receiver of Jensen Motors. The 7.2-litre Chrysler engine was no longer available, however, so Jensen Cars Ltd had to settle for the small-block Chrysler 5.9-litre engine. This engine was still very powerful though, and met all the then-current US emission control standards, which was always a plus point, and a very good reason for sticking with American engines, at least from a marketing point of view, if not from a performance one. Another point was that a fuel-injection system had been developed for this engine, which offered easier starting, greater smoothness and slightly better fuel economy. Jensen thus offered this as an option.

Remembering that the Interceptor body had originally been designed and built in Italy as far back as 1966/67, there were quite a number of items that were either unsuitable or unavailable. Indeed there were around 1000 detail changes to the specification, an important example being the door handles. The original design would not conform with current safety regulations – the S4's were thus fitted with a completely new design which looked much more modern as well as solving the problem.

Throughout the years of Interceptor production, the heating and ventilation system had never been entirely satisfactory, even with air conditioning fitted. This was another area that was improved and developed for the Series Four. Electrically adjustable front seats by Recaro were to become standard equipment. Recaro would sell the bare frames to Jensen, who would then upholster them in the finest leather to the customer's specification. The very best quality Wilton carpet had always been offered on Interceptors, but this was now extended into the boot area. The exhaust system was now stainless

A dashboard shell about to be fitted.

The front spoiler being fitted to current Interceptors.

steel, as standard equipment. The same very pretty GKN alloy wheels were specified, but with 215/VR15 tyres instead of the 205/VR15s used previously.

Ian Orford's previous observations about his company echoing the early exploits of Richard and Alan Jensen, offering the customer exactly what he wanted, were well founded. The Series Four was built to the customer's specification; paint colour, interior trim and upholstery specification, fuel injected engine, in-car entertainment, security systems, even body style, were at the whim of the customer. As well as this, Orford's team were also introducing improvements to the S4, genuine improvements, designed to bring the Interceptor into the eighties, with safety, function and style in mind.

In early 1987 the front end was restyled very slightly, the grille and head-lamp surrounds being brought forward to give a flush fitting frontal aspect. The car still looked the same, but on closer inspection, the frontal area was obviously much more modern. A front spoiler was designed with the help of various aerodynamic experts, to prevent the front end's lifting at high speeds. The spoiler was not just made of plastic and bolted on – it was fabricated in steel, welded to the lower front valence, and carefully blended in to the surrounding metal with lead. It was the same with the newly introduced rear high-intensity fog warning lights, they were to become an integral part of the bodywork, mounted just below the rear bumper. It was Jensen of old, pure craftmanship offering the customer just what he wanted. This was illustrated when, in early 1987, a customer stated that he liked the rear lines and boot area of the convertible model more than the traditional saloon styling. The only problem was that he did not want a convertible. Jensen satisfied his demand by styling a new Hard-Top model, with the required rear-end styling, and a roof! So far, only one of this striking-looking model has been built, in red, with black leather upholstery, but it showed that Jensen were now producing what the Continental press dubbed, 'The most exclusive car in the world'.

When asked about current production levels, Ian Orford was of the opinion, "Our present workload at Jensen Cars seems to vary between restoration and the new cars quite nicely. Suffice to say, most of our workers are required to work overtime around 50 per cent of the available time, which indicates that we have our 'mix' just about right. At the moment we require 6 months to produce a new car, and as regards the success or otherwise of the new cars, this is of course totally connected with the amount of advertising that we do. For instance, given, say, £10,000 to run a small campaign in a few weekly or monthly 'glossies', we could probably pick up four or five sales, maybe more. Our problem is that when we worked out the date for delivery, and then informed the customer, we would inevitably lose three or four of them. A 'Catch-22' situation that every small volume manufacturer faces. As it is, it is better for us to quietly continue receiving the odd request and turning it into a positive sale.'

In 1987 Ian Orford was involved in discussions with various consortia with the intention of discovering the viability of putting an all-new Jensen model into series production and the building of a new factory for this purpose. There were contacts with various government agencies, to discuss funding and suitable factory sites, potential agents, dealers and importers in the US, and even some styling drawings and mock-ups were made. No decision was reached, however, even though there was considerable press comment and speculation at the time.

It was Ian's intention to ensure Jensen's long term future, which he believed was inextricably tied in with new Jensen vehicles of one form or another. He explained: 'Without new cars in quantity, the level of activity will continue to diminish year by year, until it becomes economically unviable to keep and support a 'factory' of any size. Unfortunately, what it probably means for us to get a new Jensen on the road in quantity is that the investment necessary would mean a new management team, skilled in shaping a new product which carries an old and respected name. With the best will in the world, myself and my colleagues are not the right team for that job – we do not have these skills, even though no doubt there would be middle management type positions we could fill with success. Many people say to me now, "But you started the new Jensens off and running, how can you not be a part of any new company with a new car?" – to which I would have to answer, for a new company to be successful (which we all want it to be), in such a high profile, highly professional business, it must have the right people at the top, and they must be people that have done it before, because there are no second chances in this business, as we found out in 1976!'

Ian's prediction would not come true until January 1989 when Jensen Cars Ltd was sold to Unicon Holdings, that company now owning 100 per cent of the new Jensen Car Company Ltd.

It was the intention of the new Chairman of the Jensen Car Company, Hugh Wainwright, to begin development of a new model almost immediately. The new car was envisaged as having to be obviously a Jensen Interceptor, but an Interceptor for the 1990s. Provisional ideas call for a very advanced technical specification, with perhaps a very powerful American V8 encompassing the latest in fuel injection and engine management systems. It is intended that the rear chassis/floorpan area be heavily modified allowing increased leg and head room for rear seat passengers and a new independent rear suspension system.

Hugh Wainwright sees production starting at a rate of 25 cars per year. However, it is not intended that more than 50 cars a year will ever be produced. Again, the new company is not forgetting owners of older Jensen models, and the famous 'factory' restoration service will continue uninterrupted. An interesting addition is the Special Restoration Package which will bring a MkIII or S4 Interceptor up to the most modern specification.

The new car is to be introduced at the 1989 Motorfair, and further publicity for the Jensen marque is assured with the news that the latest Series Four Interceptor is to star in London Weekend Television's new series of two-hour tele-movies *The Saint*, based on the books of Leslie Charteris and starring Simon Dutton as Simon Templar. The producer of the series, Christopher Neame was recorded as saying that, 'A Jensen has the kind of quality one would expect in a car that Simon Templar might drive.'

And that sums it up: Jensen was always at the forefront of motor vehicle technology and styling; it still is, and as before, quality is uncompromised.

11

The Jensen Owner's Club

THE CAR ENTHUSIAST who owns a Jensen of any age would be well advised to join the Jensen Owners' Club, if only for the excellent stock of spare parts that the club holds, going back as far as the earliest Interceptor and 541 models. Although the original aim was to cater for the spares requirements of 541 and C-V8 owners, the club has developed over the years into an enthusiasts' social club, letting members get together to talk about their favourite motor cars and avail themselves of the numerous other benefits that JOC membership brings.

It was just before Christmas in December 1971 that a small group of enthusiasts met at the Cirencester home of Mr Alexander Kok. Just over 30 Jensens were present at this meeting, its intention being to find out if there would be enough Jensen owners interested in forming a new club, and if a club were formed, exactly what its function would be, and what it could offer to its members. A Committee was appointed and a set of rules drawn up (based upon the rules of the Singer Car Club).

By September 1972, the new club had attracted some 140 members, but these early days were very shaky, and the Jensen Owners' Club was in danger of fading into obscurity by the beginning of 1973. The Committee had stated that it was their intention to produce a newsletter every two months and a proper colour magazine every six months. This had been rather optimistic, as by the beginning of 1973 there had only been one newsletter, but the second one came out in March. This very late newsletter had in its contents a number of letters from irate members, one from member no 3, Mr Peter Wallis, who said to the General Secretary: 'I know only too well we have our differences, but take action now, call a meeting and let's start again before it's too late. We obviously have a number of people who are far more capable than the present Committee.'

Over the remaining months of 1973 much progress was made. The original Committee was still pretty much the same; one or two had resigned, and a few new posts were formed. By October the fourth newsletter had been delivered to members, this one being the first produced by professional printers, the previous newsletters being simple duplicated sheets stapled together. The editor informed the membership that their number was now over 240 — the Jensen Owners' Club had pulled its socks up and was now going places!

By February 1974, the club had put together a list of members' cars: there were 2 members that owned pre-war cars; 1 member owned a PW Saloon; the

Shields and cups awaiting to be awarded at the annual Jensen Owners' Club International Weekend.

All Jensen models are catered for by the JOC, from this PW model . . .

. . . through the 541 Series . . .

. . . to the ever-popular Jensen-Healey.

A Swedish FF at an inter-club meeting.

original Interceptor accounted for 9 members; 62 members owned a 541; another 48 owned 541-Rs; the 541-S model accounted for 25 owners; the C-V8s, 56 members; the new Interceptor owners were now starting to join the JOC: 20 owners had now become club members, 4 of them owning FFs; the Jensen-Healey had now been in proper series production for just over a year, and at this stage only one owner had joined the JOC.

The social side of the JOC was starting to become established. There had been a tentative attempt at a national get-together in June 1973, with the JOC Rally at Beaulieu. This was quite successful, and included a concours competition which was only open to owners of Jensens up to the 541-R, with another class for owners of 541-S models and C-V8s. In 1974, the National Rally was held at the Chequers Hotel in Blackpool, over the weekend of June 8/9. This was the beginning of a tradition in the JOC, that the most important event of the year would be the National Rally, later called the International Weekend, and that this would bring together members from all corners of the globe, with a common aim and interest.

Towards the end of 1977, due to the ever increasing size of the Club, both in terms of finances and membership, it was agreed by the Committee that a Limited Company should be formed, to take over the obligations, assets, liabilities and the general conduct of the club. The company was to be called the Jensen Owners' Club Limited, and was formed to protect the club members and their Committee. The Company was limited by guarantee and the current membership were not asked to contribute further than their normal subscriptions. By the end of 1981, however, with the club membership still increasing, and also the price of a year's subscription increasing, the club were faced with an ever increasing payment to Her Majesty's Government for Value Added Tax. This was now 15 per cent of the club's gross turnover, and obviously this situation could not be allowed to go on forever. Consequently, an Extraordinary General Meeting of the JOC Ltd was called on the 13th of December that year. It was decided to split the club into two separate entities: the Jensen Owners' Club Ltd., a company formed to sell Jensen spares and club regalia etc, and an unincorporated members' social club, to be known as the Jensen Owners' Club. This managed to stabilize the club's finances, and they looked forward to the 1980s with increased optimism.

Today the total membership of approximately 1250 members around the world has the majority of members owning Interceptors and Jensen-Healeys, the spares service is stronger and better organised than ever, and the club is recognised as being in the forefront of British motoring clubs. The favourite event that the JOC organise is still the International Weekend; usually held in the second week of June, the JOC takes over a suitable large hotel from the Friday to the Sunday evening. On the Saturday, the remainder of members arrive, and the club's Annual General Meeting is held in the morning, which gives the ordinary club member the chance to have a say in club affairs. In the afternoon, there are technical discussions, coach trips to the surrounding areas and other social events organised to keep the members interested and amused. For many, the highlight of the weekend is the dinner-dance held on the Saturday evening.

The Concours is held on the Sunday, and this particular event is taken very seriously by the contestants, and the standards of preparation and condition of the Jensens on show is rising every year. The Jensen Owners' Club is fortunate to have a number of members' cars that have been prepared to world class concours standards and there are always guaranteed to be a few gasps of amazement when the bonnet is lifted on one of these examples. With the large commercially organised concours competitions that have become popular in the UK in recent years, there are many owners of many different marques of classic cars that have brought their cars to a very high standard, but the cars of the JOC are always to be found in the last round of finalists.

The Jensen Owners' Club is a very professionally run organisation and this is illustrated by the number of members that have stayed with the club over the years, quite a few after they have sold their Jensens! It has always been known as a very friendly club, and the members of the Executive Committee very approachable. It is not unusual at the International Weekend to see the Chairman advising a member on his car's originality, the General Secretary giving away a few secrets on concours preparation to a member that he has not met before, or the Magazine Editor advising a new member on how to rectify his paintwork problems. Part of the enjoyment of owning a Jensen is being involved with the Jensen Owners' Club, and members from all over the United Kingdom are catered for, with strong local area sections.

Jensen Clubs around the World

The interest in preserving and enjoying all models of Jensens is a hobby of worldwide proportions, with clubs in Germany, Australia, the USA, Japan and Sweden.

In Sweden they are known as the Swedish Jensen Drivers' Club, and at present they have just over 150 members, about two-thirds owning Interceptors. The Jensen Owners' Club of Japan so far only has seven members, but with about 50 Jensens in Japan they are growing steadily.

In Germany, the Jensen Owners' Club of Germany was founded in late 1983, and enthusiastically support their 'donner und blitzen' machines!

The Jensen Interceptor Car Club, based in Victoria, looks after enthusiasts' interests in Australia. It publishes a busy and informative magazine, named *The Interceptor*.

In the United States, the major club is the Association of Jensen Owners, based on the east coast. The AJO came about after discussions in late 1976 between Mike Lotwis, Hal Kendall and Gary Selman, and the club effectively came into being at the beginning of 1977. In July of that year they published the first issue of *The White Lady*, their news journal, this magazine flourishing through the years, with a much more technical bias than the British offering. The Honorary President of the AJO was none other than Kjell Qvale himself, and he was obviously pleased to fulfil this post, as he wrote in *The White Lady*, issue number one:

'It is an honour and a pleasure for me to become the Honorary President of the Association of Jensen Owners. The economics of the day and the peculiar problems in Great Britain have worked together to eliminate from the marketplace a wonderful automobile industry. It is a sad thing to happen, but at the same time, it is following in the footsteps of many other illustrious cars. From an enthusiast's standpoint, there are some minor pluses in this development which can be found through the added enjoyment of owning and

German Jensens at the Nürburgring, 1985.
Jensens at an Australian club meeting.

The AJO looks after the interests of American east-coast owners.

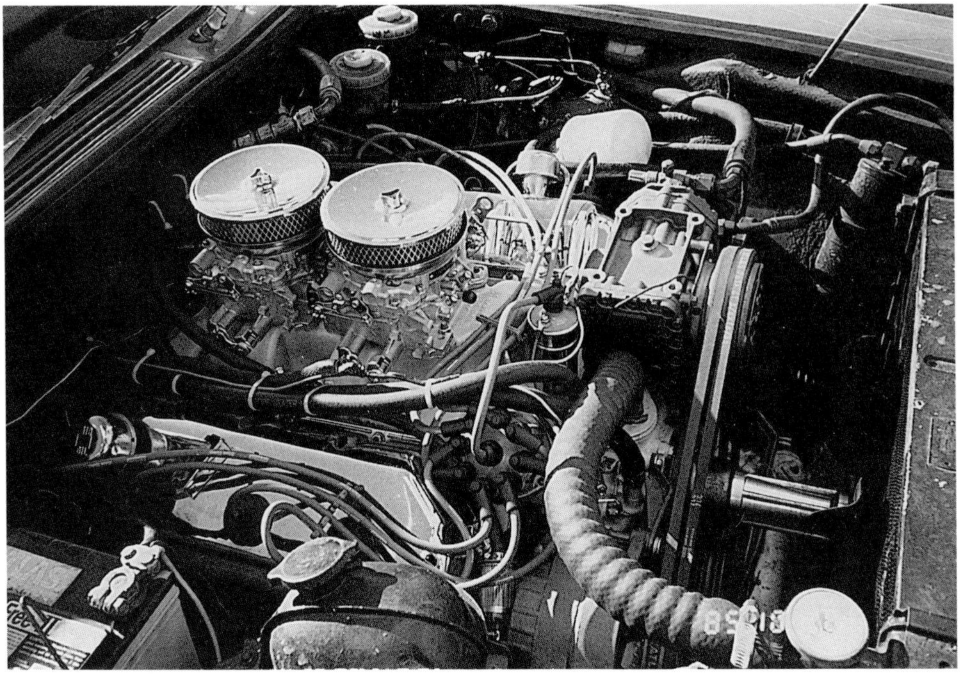

The engine-bay of an American Interceptor, fitted with a 426ci Hemi engine and dual 4-barrel carburettors.

Enthusiastic Californian club members.

driving a special car that will become increasingly desirable as time goes on and the numbers slowly diminish.

'I hope the Jensens that all of you own perform in a satisfactory manner and I want to assure all of you that we intend to keep spare parts flowing as long as they are needed.'

The AJO has a close association with the British JOC, and there is usually a strong contingent of AJO members present at every Jensen Owners' Club International Weekend.

The west coast of the USA is served by both the Sacramento Area Jensen Owners' Club and the Jensen Interceptor Owners' Club, both of which cater for owners of Jensen models of any age. The JIOC produces a regular magazine entitled *Gentleman's Express,* and although smaller in content than either the British Jensen Owners' Club magazine or *The White Lady*, the *Gentleman's Express* echoes the enthusiasm of Jensen owners throughout the world.

The memory of the motor cars originally designed by the Jensen brothers will live on as long as there are enthusiasts and their clubs, and with a new car waiting in the wings, the name Jensen should also live on for many years to come.

Index